Bollywood Showplaces

Bollywood Showplaces

Cinema Theatres in India

David Vinnels and Brent Skelly

Additional material on Rajasthan by Braj Raj Singh

E & E Plumridge Ltd, Cambridge

in collaboration with Decorum Books, London

First published in 2002 by
E & E Plumridge Ltd
41 High Street
Linton
Cambridge CB1 6HS

Produced in collaboration with and distributed by
Decorum Books
24 Cloudesley Square
London N1 OHN

email decorumbooks@tiscali.co.uk

ISBN 0-9516563-5-X

Frontispiece: *Attendant at the Odeon, New Delhi*

Contents

Acknowledgements

The authors wish to thank the many individuals and organisations that assisted with the research and writing of this book. The managers and owners of the cinemas visited generously provided information and extensive tours of the buildings. Special mention must be made of the contributions of Mrs Gertrude Barucha of the Edward Theatre, Mumbai; Mr P. Chaphalkar of the Mangala, Pune; Mr S. Dayal of the Regal, New Delhi; Mr N. Hoosein and Mr Lobo of the Liberty, Mumbai; Mr S. K. Golcha of the Golcha Group of Jaipur; Mr Sudher Kasliwal of the Gem, Jaipur; Mr D. C. & Mr U. D. Kaushish of the Shiela, New Delhi; Mr Sanjeev Khandelwal of the Metro, Kolkata; Mr Ranesh Khanna of the Chanakya, New Delhi; Mr S. Kirpal of the Umaid Bhavan Palace Hotel, Jodhpur, Mr & Mrs J. Mantosh of the New Empire & Lighthouse, Kolkata; Mr R. K. Modi of Western India Theatres Ltd, Mumbai; Mr S. J. Mukherjee of the Globe, Kolkata; Mr Om Prakash and Mr A. Shama of the Polo Victory, Jaipur; Mr B. N. Sahni of the Odeon, New Delhi; Mr Samabh Saxena of Priva Village Roadshow Ltd., New Delhi; Mr M. F. Sidhwa of Globe Theatres Ltd, Mumbai; Messrs Surana of the Raj Mandir, Jaipur and Mr K. Venugopl of the Shanti, Chennai. Amongst many architects who provided both background information and details of their own buildings, we are particularly indebted to Mr Sarbit Singh Bahga, Mr Surinder Singh Bagha, Mr Satish H. Kadam, Mr Vijay Malik, Mr Prakash N. Mathur, Mr Rahul Mehrotra, Mr Aditya Prakash and Mr Shiv Nath Prasad all of whom generously responded to numerous queries over many months. Architectural and historical reference material was made available by Mr Rafique Baghdadi of Mumbai, Mr Mustafa K. Chand of Chennai, Mr B. K. Nair of Pune, Mr T. K. Sathyu of Kolkata, Mr Ken Sutcliffe of Guildford and Mr Jon Alff of California. Mr Charles Pitt of Nogent-sur-Maine provided information about early theatres and opera in India. Of the numerous archives, libraries and collections consulted, in London, the British Film Institute, the Library of The High Commission of India and the Royal Institute of British Architects were especially helpful. In India, the National Film Archive of India in Pune and the Indian Institute of Architects in Mumbai both made available what references they hold dealing specifically with cinema buildings and the former also provided significant background information about the industry. Mr D. F. Hodiwalla of the Liberty, Pune and the Cinematograph Exhibitors' Association of India, Mumbai, helped with statistics. Mr Mosul Azaad and Mr Bharat Upadhayaya put their extensive knowledge of Delhi at our disposal as did Dr N. S. Rangarju in Mysore and Mr A. K. Saha in Kolkata. Professor Kiran Joshi and Dr I. J. S. Bakshi at the Chandigarh School of Architecture supplied information about that city. In London, Mr Nigel Quiney and Mr David Evans made available their collection of Indian cinema advertisements. During the two years working on the book, Mr Julian Holland put his exceptional professional experience at our disposal, offering invaluable support, criticism and advice and in the weeks before he died, together with his wife Carole, scrutinised the text to root out solecisms. Most importantly, without the apparently inexhaustible enthusiasm, contacts and organisational skills of Mr Harish Chopra of New Delhi our research visits to India would have been far less fruitful and not anywhere near as enjoyable.

Picture Credits: All illustrations are from photographs by the authors, their collection of cinema ephemera or material made available by cinema owners and managers, except for the cinema advertisements from the collection of Nigel Quiney and David Evans, Mustafa K. Chand, p122; Charles Pitt collection, p119, Shiv Nath Prasad, p42; Sarbit Singh Bahga, p272; Ken Sutcliffe, p23, p84 (left), p88, p90 (right); Willard & Co., p99 (bottom). Whilst every effort has been made to trace copyright holders, we apologise for any errors or omissions and would be glad to be notified of these so that corrections can be made in any reprint.

Preface

The cinema theatre in India, its development, history, design and associated personalities, is the subject of this book. For several decades now, the Indian film industry has been the largest in the world. Its economic, social and artistic significance is already being researched and a considerable literature is in existence concerning the film stars and directors, the fans and the productions; detailed analyses are available of at least some of the films. Little attention, however, has been paid to the other important constituent of the business, namely cinema exhibition. Yet, the venue, where the paying customer voluntarily chooses to view a film projected on to a full-size screen, is the touchstone by which the success or failure of the entire industry is largely measured.

The book sets out to explore the first century of Indian film exhibition by tracing the individual stories of some one hundred cinemas and recording their current appearance and technical equipment. In a country so vast, the choice of possible locales and cinemas is almost overwhelming. We decided, therefore, to restrict the scope of this volume to a relatively small number of cities but, in order to provide a reasonably balanced picture overall, every type of commercial movie theatre was researched, from well-known and popular city-centre cinemas to small, back street and rundown suburban ones, as well as a few multiplexes. However, the eventual selection included in the book is somewhat biased, insofar as older cinemas, particularly those with uncertain futures, have to some extent been favoured at the expense of more recent single-screen and multiplex venues. Space, though, has been found for several long-closed establishments as well as a few demolished venues and ones that never got far beyond the drawing board.

The twelve cities selected are spread across the country. First are the four great metropolitan conurbations - Mumbai (Bombay), Kolkata (Calcutta) and Chennai (Madras), which were the most important commercial centres during the British period and until 1911, Calcutta was also the capital of British India, together with Delhi, which includes the new capital, New Delhi. Next, two former hill stations: Shimla (Simla) built on an Himalayan ridge, the summer seat of Government in the British time and now a holiday resort and Pune (Poona), which since Independence has been transformed into an educational centre with a thriving information technology industry. The former Princely Cities are represented by Hyderabad, like Pune, a major I.T. centre; three cities in the State of Rajasthan - Jaipur, Jodhpur and Bikaner - and in the south one further example - Mysore. The last choice fell on Chandigarh, the capital of Punjab State, a new city created since Independence.

Primary sources and even any reliable secondary references specific to the origins and early history of cinema and theatre buildings in India are exceptionally scant and do not figure prominently in any of the relevant archives. Furthermore, what little information is available is often incomplete or contradictory and important facts such as names of architects and designers or opening and conversion dates have in many cases, apparently, not been recorded. Most exhibitors have no systematic archives upon which to draw and, in many instances, the bulk of their records and ephemera have either been lost or destroyed. A few exhibitors, however, have retained important historical documentation, but as paper is not treated kindly by the Indian climate, this is more often than not in a poor state of preservation or exists only in the form of old and fading photocopies.

Much of the material upon which this book is based was obtained during extensive interviews with owners and managers of cinemas in the course of visits undertaken over the last two years. Information given about the venues, architecture and history of the buildings along with unlimited access to every part of the cinema, provided a unique insight into the workings of film exhibition in India today. The overriding impression given was of time running out for many existing venues and numerous owners, alert to the threat posed by new technologies, predicted radical changes in the way films will be exhibited in the country in the future. Moreover, we were repeatedly warned not expect a high percentage of the cinemas visited to still be in business in ten years time. By now, several of the venues described in the book have already been drastically altered; others have closed awaiting demolition.

Before embarking upon this project, we were asked by an architectural historian in India, "Why travel all this way to see horrible, Indian lower middle-class, kitsch culture when you could look at over six thousand years of our great architecture?". What is described and illustrated here will go some way, we hope, to providing an answer to this question and explain why we believe such buildings are not only worthy of research but in some instances, preservation.

Our principal objective is to stimulate interest in the subject, especially within India itself, and to help identify and document some of the most architecturally and historically important cinemas in the country. This is a first look at the subject; there remain many gaps in the story to be explored, numerous cinemas still to be documented and further research is needed to discover more about the histories of the exhibitors themselves and careers of the architects and the designers. Cinemas played a significant role in the popular culture of twentieth-century India: they represent an important manifestation of that heritage. Our hope is that this book will increase appreciation of what remains before still more is swept away and lost forever.

David Vinnels and Brent Skelly, London, May 2002

Historical Note

The history of cinema in India encompasses two periods: the colonial era of the British Raj and, following Partition in 1947, Independence. Partition created two new Dominions, India and Pakistan, which both later became Republics. This book is concerned solely with cinemas within the boundaries of present-day India.

During the British period, India comprised two worlds: British India, divided into Provinces headed by a Governor and subject to a Viceroy representing the British Crown, and some six hundred and fifty Princely States, which governed over a quarter of the whole population and nearly half the land mass. Each of these States had its own hereditary Ruler, who acknowledged British paramountcy; after Independence, all were absorbed either into India or Pakistan.

Democratic India is subdivided into States formed by amalgamating Princely States with parts of the former British Provinces. Several cities formerly within British India have undergone changes of name and the former city name is used when historically appropriate. Streets have also been subject to successive re-namings over the years and, with the exception of cinemas that continue to use a previous street name as their formal address or in their advertising, current official street names are indicated.

Where population figures are quoted, they are approximations taking account of the provisional results of the 2001 Census. Owing to the large numbers living in the cities without fixed abode, these figures should be treated with caution.

← *The Liberty, Mumbai, built 1947-50.*

Part One

1. Cinema Comes to India

Scroll paintings, illuminated and dramatised sequentially to the accompaniment of a vocal chant or instrumental music, were a traditional means of storytelling in India. Such routines were used in temples to retell the familiar tales of Gods and Goddesses for the mostly illiterate worshippers - comparable, no doubt, with the role played by stained glass in mediaeval churches in Europe. In similar fashion, to animate folk tales entertainers would hold up a series of hand-drawn pictures or cut-outs, sometimes incorporating puppets into the act as well, and thereby create the illusion of movement. Storytelling accompanied by such simple devices was a part of many showmen's stock-in-trade long before any sophisticated projection equipment was obtainable.

However, once the magic lantern or slide projector became widely available in the country during the nineteenth century, it was then possible using painted glass slides to show pictures many times enlarged by projecting the image on to a screen. These presentations proved extremely popular and being portable could be set up almost anywhere, even in the open air after dark. Indian audiences favoured elaborate mythological and historical adventures involving the fantastic and the supernatural. For example, in a show illustrating scenes from an epic drama such as *Mahabharata*, a narrator might recite the story as a counterpoint to the projected images, whilst actors or dancers mimed choreographed movements and musicians supplied an atmospheric background harmony. Europeans, on the other hand, were much more inclined to want programmes consisting of comedies, factual stories and travelogues. By the end of the century, most lanternists in the big cities were showing photographic slides, having abandoned hand-painted images which by then were thought rather old-fashioned. In rural areas, however, these continued in use for considerably longer.

The introduction of a quick change or dissolve between two or more related slides enabled the showmen to present transformations of size, scale and positions of figures and scenes far

← *An advertisement in* The Times of India *in 1870 for magic lantern equipment and slides.*

more fluently: a procedure exploiting the phenomenon known as "persistence of vision," whereby an image is momentarily retained beyond the time actually viewed and a rapid sequence of related pictures is perceived as an unbroken continuity – the fundamental contrivance, in fact, of all motion picture imagery. And so, when cinematic film actually arrived in the country, no great leap of imagination was required on the part of the audience to accept either the element of magic or the simulacrum of movement generated by the new medium. The Indian public's first response to moving pictures was ecstatic, but apparently accompanied by none of the scenes of startled amazement recorded in Europe. As the film archivist P. K. Nair reports:

> …the new phenomenon did not create much of a stir here and none in the audience ran out at the image of a train speeding towards them, as they did elsewhere. The Indian viewer took the cinematic experience in his stride as something already familiar to him.[1]

Projected moving pictures resulted from the marriage of photography with various technological developments during the latter half of the 19th century. Several early devices used glass or flexible discs, others employed cylinders, as a base to support a sequence of photographic pictures; however, all these systems were eventually superseded by the introduction of flexible cellulose nitrate film. When engaged by a suitable shift mechanism, a strip of film could be advanced intermittently and extremely accurately past a shutter, thereby allowing a succession of individual pictures or frames to be either photographed or illuminated and if the frequency was identical in both instances, the images apparently reproduced natural movement.

During the last decade of the nineteenth century, inventors in several countries including America, Britain and France were simultaneously but independently working to perfect just such a moving picture apparatus. When Auguste and Louis Lumière demonstrated their

→ *The announcement in* The Times of India *of the first presentation of the Lumière Brothers' 'Cinématographe' on 7th July 1896 at Watson's Hotel, Bombay.*

THE MARVEL OF THE CENTURY.
THE WONDER OF THE WORLD.
LIVING PHOTOGRAPHIC PICTURES
IN
LIFE-SIZED REPRODUCTIONS
BY
MESSRS. LUMIERE BROTHERS.
CINEMATOGRAPHE.
A FEW EXHIBITIONS WILL BE GIVEN
AT
WATSON'S HOTEL
TO-NIGHT (7TH instant).
PROGRAMME will be as under:

1. Entry of Cinematographe.
2. Arrival of a Train.
3. The Sea Bath.
4. A Demolition
5. Leaving the Factory.
6. Ladies and Soldiers on Wheels.

The Entertainment will take place at 6, 7, 9, and 10 p.m.

ADMISSION ONE RUPEE.

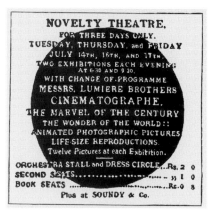

EXCELSIOR
CINEMATOGRAPH,
NOVELTY THEATRE.

TO-NIGHT
GREAT SPORTING ATTRACTION,
THE CUP
FINAL.
Newcastle United vs. Bradford City.
The Match at the
Crystal Palace
and the
Replay
Come and see this great film
THE DANCER OF SIVA
A wonderful coloured film founded
On an old Hindu Legend
M. PRINCE
Is a screaming absurdity
and
Other popular pictures

TO-MORROW,
SUNDAY,
GRAND PRIZE SHOW.
7 to 8 p.m.
One Gold Watch and Two Silver
Watches given away.

Time and Prices as usual.
The Excelsior Garden is the
Coolest Spot in the City.
The Rendezvous of Bombay.

NEW TENT-MAIDAN

Elphinstone Bioscope.
TO-DAY
2 PERFORMANCES 2
at 6-15 p.m. and 9-30 p.m

ELPHINSTONE PRESENTS   For the First Time in India.
"SATYAWADI RAJA
HARISCHANDRA
The Great Dramatic Success of the Indian Stage. Adapted for the screen from
the famous drama of the same name and featuring.

THE EMOTIONAL STAR—MISS SAVARIA
and supported by the "Irving" of the Indian Stage
MR. HORMUSJEE TANTRA
and the Baliwala Victoria Theatrical Co. of Bombay.
Produced under the sole supervision of The Elphinstone Bioscope Co. of Calcutta.

SATYAWADI RAJA HARISCHANDRA
In 5 Reels—7,000 Feet Long

This play, which has had a most successful run on the Indian Stage for the
last forty years. It is a play which pictures.
THE LIFE OF A HINDU KING
who, surrounded by all the grandeur and luxury that wealth could give, yet lived
the life of nobility and purity, to whom falsehood and injustice were as strangers
and whose very virtues excited the wonder and the envy of the Gods above.

SATYAWADI RAJA HARISCHANDRA
AN ALL-ELPHINSTONE PHOTO-PLAY
Also in addition to the above film masterpiece a sensational and thrilling drama
entitled.
"FOR THE SAKE OF HER CHILD"   Produced by the "DANMARK FILM CO"
In Three Reels—4,000 Feet Long,   Will be screened for the first time in India

'Cinématographe' on 28th December 1895 at the Salon Indien of the Grand Café in Paris, it was the first public presentation before a paying audience of a moving film projected on to a screen – in effect, the start of commercial cinema exhibition.

Barely six months after this initial demonstration in Paris, the 'Cinématographe' reached India. The first film show was given on 7th July 1896 at a temporary auditorium set up in Watson's Hotel in Bombay, after which the programmes continued at the Novelty Theatre for a few more weeks. Rival operators such as Stewart's 'Vitagraph', Hughe's 'Motoscope', The Charles Urban Trading Co. Ltd. and The Warwick Trading Co. Ltd. soon arrived in the country thus ensuring cinematic exhibition continued, albeit intermittently, during the next few years.

At first, projection equipment was installed on a temporary basis in a few drama and variety theatres in Bombay, Calcutta and Madras. Treated in the theatrical world as, at best, a gimmick, films were usually only included in stage shows by promoters wishing to inject some variety into a magic act or as a *divertissement* in the interval of a play, but with each item running a minute or less, the programmes were little more than a series of unrelated short incidents. The more enterprising venues filmed short sequences of their own live productions and as competition to the theatres, photographic studios made their own programmes of short moving films. Magic lanternists, however, were quick to appreciate the possibilities of the new medium: an attraction that could be incorporated easily into their existing shows. Presentations were soon being included in many of the entertainments offered by these showmen,

← (top) *The announcement in* The Times of India *in July 1896 of the first 'Cinématographe' shows at the Novelty Theatre, Bombay.*

←← *An advertisement in* The Times of India *in May 1911 for a special programme promoted by the cinema entrepreneurs Excelsior Cinematograph at the Novelty Theatre, comprising a newsreel film of the recent F. A. Cup Final followed by a programme including an Indian mythological drama. Later, the theatre was known by both its original name, Novelty, and also as the Excelsior – the later name eventually superseding the earlier one. In the advertisement, the theatre garden is already being referred to as the Excelsior Garden.*

← *An advertisement dated 1917 for one of J. F. Madan's Elphinstone Bioscope tented shows in Calcutta. The film,* Harischandra, *was an Elphinstone production – a remake of Dada Saheb Phalke's* Raja Harischandra, *the first full-length feature film made in India.*

who, for the most part, operated in tents on the maidans - the grassed swards in the centre of the big cities. Concurrently, itinerant entertainers, conjurors and puppeteers began to take up the invention introducing a number of film sequences into their acts as an additional treat to the usual fare. Armed with a projector, folding screen and some cans of film, they travelled around the country in horse-drawn carts, at each stop setting up a rudimentary cinema in a tent or the open air.

By 1899, the word 'Bioscope' had been coined to describe both the venue as well as the entertainment itself and it was not long before some astute businesses were including it in their trading names. The British, surprisingly, played a minor role in the early development of film production and exhibition in India, which left the way clear for Indian showmen and entrepreneurs to exploit the potential of the new medium. One such was Abdulally Esoofally. He was reported in the early 1900s as operating a tent cinema in Bombay measuring some 30-metres x 15-metres supported on four pillars, with a staff of twenty-five and able to accommodate an audience of over a thousand. Esoofally's later partner, A. M. Irani, J. F. Madan in Calcutta and F. H. Sidhwa and his partner K. A. Kooka in Rangoon and later Calcutta were comparable pioneers: that the nascent Indian film industry developed so rapidly was due to the efforts of men such as these. But whilst the British stood aside in the early years of the twentieth century, the French firm Pathé Frères established a presence in Bombay to distribute films and sell stock and equipment and in 1916, Hollywood's Universal Picture Corporation followed suit, becoming the first American studio to open an office in the country. Cinema exhibition, although continuing to expand, was an *ad hoc* affair until the first permanent cinemas started operating in Calcutta in the early 1900s and soon after in Madras and Bombay. Initially, no new buildings were constructed; instead, existing European-style drama and variety theatres were converted. This development notwithstanding, tented shows proliferated, for a long time seemingly unaffected by the new competition and only gradually disappeared from urban areas over the following two decades.

2. Theatres into Cinemas

Quite when the first European theatre was established in India is uncertain, but one of the earliest was the Playhouse in Calcutta built in 1745 and some twenty-five years later a similar theatre opened in Bombay. Over the next fifty years or so, the story of theatre in India was full of failures and false starts and theatrical ventures were not a success to any significant extent until the second half of the nineteenth century. Then, the situation suddenly changed: numerous, indigenous production companies flourished, the most successful playing in substantial theatres in the major cities. At the same time, European audiences were catered for by local and in all probability mostly amateur drama groups and touring variety acts performing in English. Troupes from Europe presenting seasons of drama and opera were a particular attraction in Bombay, Calcutta and Madras.

A number of these early theatre buildings are still extant having been converted into full-time cinemas. The Grant Road Theatre (now Gulshan Talkies) in Bombay opened in 1853, the Edward in 1860, followed soon after by the Ripon (now Alfred Talkies) and the grandest of all, the Gaiety (now Capitol) in 1879. In Calcutta, performances at the Opera House (now Globe) started during the 1860s. Many of these buildings, Baroque or classical in appearance, were much like comparable establishments of the period in Britain but in instances such as the Star and the Rubani in Calcutta or the Sheekrishna and Shee Chmundshweri at Mysore, their European designs were embellished by the introduction of either Hindu or, more usually, Mughal details like *chajjas*, *jalis* and *chhatris*.

Elsewhere, other influences are apparent. In Jaipur, behind a long terrace typical of the city, the exterior of the Ramprakash of 1878 has the appearance of an Italian basilica. At the Gaiety of 1887 in Simla, an auditorium like that of a small Italian opera house lies hidden inside an austere Gothic exterior. However, apart from this example, Gothic was not widely used for theatre building; nor was Indo-Saracenic – the attempt by British architects to adopt an Indian Revivalist idiom. During the early years of the twentieth century, more lavish Baroque and Rococo decorative treatments found favour with theatrical managements: the crowning monument of that era is, undoubtedly, the imposing Royal Opera House in Bombay, which dates from 1910.

New theatres continued to be constructed well into the 1930s, but a less ornate, stripped classicism gradually replaced these more elaborate styles: the Opera DeLuxe in Mysore and the Empire (now Roxy Talkies) in Calcutta were built in the 1920s. Following the move of the Imperial Capital from Calcutta to Delhi in 1911, the new city saw many venues inaugurated after its official completion in the late l920s: the Roxy (now Minerva), the New Amar and the Imperial all opened in the early 1930s. By then, Bombay, Calcutta, Madras and Delhi, were well served by theatres offering either 'native' drama in one of the Indian languages or English productions. Smaller cities could probably account for no more than one or two, although in an influential and wealthy Princely City like Mysore, four such venues were operating by the mid-1920s. What is surprising, though, is that so many of these theatres are major landmarks, yet the names of the architects who designed them are in most cases unrecorded.

The earliest conversion of a theatre into a full-time cinema was undertaken by J. F. Madan's Elphinstone Company in Calcutta around 1907 – either the Elphinstone Picture Palace (now Chaplin) or possibly the Corinthian (demolished) – but, apparently, neither the precise date is known nor which was first. Madan soon acquired more venues and other showmen and exhibitors quickly followed his example. Thereafter, theatres grand and small, and other suitable venues or halls in cities all over the country, were either converted by their existing owners or succumbed to offers made by other promoters. An astonishing upsurge in activity lead to a large number of live theatres closing down only to reopen a short time later in the new guise

→ *The former Gaiety Theatre, Bombay, renamed the Capitol after its acquisition and transformation into a full time cinema by Sidhwa and Kooka's Globe Theatres Ltd. The pediments and mansard roofs were later removed. (From an old photostat)*

→ *The monumental gatehouse of the Rubani, Kolkata. The auditorium hall, in a more pronounced Mughal style, is just visible through the grilles of the three huge window openings. The Rubani was converted into a cinema in the late 1920s and closed in 1994.*

of a cinema hall. In most of the early conversions, except for the installation of the necessary equipment and a new name sign, changes to the building were minimal. Balconies or 'gods' might be commandeered for projection cabins; sometimes side boxes were removed, often not. The orchestra pit and backstage facilities were usually retained to allow occasional live performances to continue and, should the new medium prove a failure, facilitate its return to live theatre. During these early years, one important factor in film exhibition received tardy attention - the danger of nitrate film stock – and only after a serious fire at a cinema in 1910 were any safely regulations introduced.

Theatres were converted for cinema-use throughout the first half of the century and several well-established drama houses changed over to become equally famous movie theatres. Two notable instances are the Royal Opera House in Bombay, which except for a brief period retained its original name, and the Grand Opera House in Calcutta renamed the Globe.

↑ *The Shee Chmundshweri, Mysore, is a mixture of Western and Indian architectural styles, although the auditorium is entirely classical with chaste Adam-style mouldings painted green, white and gold. The balcony and other handrails are brass, some ending as swan heads. Designed by the local practice of Boraiah & Basayaish, the Shee Chmundshweri opened in the early 1900s as a drama house and was converted for cinema use around 1920. From the small lobby, a steep flight of stairs leads up to an ambulatory at the first-floor auditorium level, where patrons are confronted by a stuffed elephant head – a trophy of a Royal hunting expedition.*

→ *The auditorium of the Royal Opera House, Bombay, showing the original side boxes that were demolished sometime after it was converted into a cinema; those at the rear of the stalls continued to be used. Although closed for over ten years, most other features are still intact. (An illustration in the Royal Opera House 1924 Souvenir Book)*

3. The Purpose-Built Cinema: Changing Styles and Fashions

The most enterprising exhibitors expanded rapidly by either opening ever more, new venues or taking over rival establishments. A number diversified into film production. Once these entrepreneurs were successfully presenting their own product, a converted theatre was no longer considered satisfactory. The time had come to construct purpose-built cinemas and it was businessmen involved in film production who were instrumental in developing the first of these.

The earliest appeared around 1914: the Gaiety in Madras, built by the father and son partnership of Raghupathi Venkaiah and Raghupati Surya Prakasha Rao, was one of the first and the (demolished) Cinema Majestic in Bombay opened in 1918 by the Essoofally-Irani Company was another. At this stage, the new purpose-built cinemas copied the standard theatrical layout, but were usually devoid of any of the architectural and decorative sophistication of the earlier buildings. Often the auditorium, set in a compound that served as an open-air foyer, was no more than a featureless, shed-like structure with a more elaborate, superimposed frontage. In Pune, both the original (demolished) West End and the Prabhat, erected in the centre of such compounds, had simple, functional auditoria behind attractive, decorated façades.

The usual three-level, theatre auditorium was abandoned from the start in favour of either a single floor layout, possibly in stadium configuration, or the more usual stalls and balcony arrangement. In several larger venues, full or partial stage facilities were still included. However, it is doubtful if architects were involved in the design of many of these early cinema buildings; more likely local craftsmen and contractors imitated what they had seen and possibly even built previously in a traditional theatre.

← *The West End, Poona, opened in 1917. Behind the decorative façade is an unadorned rectangular auditorium with verandahs along both sides for access. This building was demolished in the early 1980s and replaced by an office and hotel development with a new cinema that retained the name. (photographed in 1947)*

The first cinemas known to have been designed by architects appeared in Bombay and New Delhi. When the Pathé (demolished) opened in Bombay in 1930, it was described as the most luxurious venue in the city. Designed by David W. Ditchburn, who later worked with Thomas W. Lamb on the Metro in the same city, the Pathé was an ornate, classical building with a pedimented façade, large marble-clad foyers and a richly decorated auditorium. In New Delhi, as befitting their place in the new capital of Sir Edwin Lutyens and Sir Herbert Baker, the first new cinemas, which opened in the early 1930s, displayed a similar, sober classicism in keeping with their Imperial surroundings. Robert Tor Russell incorporated the Odeon and the Plaza into his grand colonnaded scheme for Connaught Place and nearby, Walter George, previously Baker's representative in Delhi, designed the Regal in the style of a Palladian villa. These stately structures, white rendered outside, cool and dignified within, provided suitably elegant surroundings for official and private visits by members of the British establishment.

By the 1930s, American not British films dominated Indian screens and compared with the elegance and fantasy these films portrayed, even the best city-centre establishments appeared dull and old-fashioned. In addition, the introduction of sound required a far more professional approach to auditorium design. Exhibitors realised that, in order to satisfy cinemagoers' expectations, an entirely new type of venue was needed: sophisticated, luxurious and comfortable, equipped with the latest technical facilities. Consequently, a number of Hollywood Studios commissioned or were instrumental in the development of prestigious, new American-style super cinemas in the smartest locations of Bombay and Calcutta. Strongly influenced by and in some instances designed by American architects, they brought to India a glimpse of previously undreamed of luxury and chic, with the objective, no less, of replicating something of the spectacle and glamour of the great picture houses of the United States.

→ *A corner of the Odeon, New Delhi. One of the original vertical Odeon signs is still in place between the classical columns of Robert Tor Russell's Connaught Place facade.*

Ironically, the first such super cinema in Bombay, the Regal for the Globe Theatre Company of Calcutta, was not designed by an American but by a relatively unknown British architect, Charles F. Stevens. Not long after, Thomas W. Lamb, the New York-based architect, was responsible for the design of two MGM houses, one in Calcutta the other in Bombay. Meanwhile, the Indian architect Sorabji K. Bhedwar was employing an entirely American Art Deco idiom at the Eros in Bombay. Art Deco cinemas were built in many other Indian cities; most notable were the Relief in Ahmadabad, Gujarat, (altered), the Odeon in Lucknow, Uttar Pradesh, (closed), and several in Madras (mostly demolished). Behind imposing Art Deco facades, these venues provided huge, elegant foyers for patrons to stroll and socialise before watching a film in a sumptuous, air-conditioned auditorium, fitted with the most up-to-date technical equipment. Commenting on the Bombay cinemas, the American architect Jon Alff wrote:

> The Art Deco cinema framed dramatic stories in isolated places of wonder. Simple on the exterior, like the caves of Ajanta and Ellora, the cinemas created a complex, richly layered emotional experience within. Drawing viewers into cool, darkened interiors, the Regal, Eros and Metro distanced people from the world outside and joined them with another within. While temple spaces were small and private, in contrast with the cinema's enormous, densely populated auditorium, both utilised conscious spatial and lighting devices to present personal impressions of distant worlds.

> Art Deco cinema embodied the Modern elegance and comfort depicted in films, but otherwise unavailable to most Indian audiences. Movie viewers experienced uniquely Modern perceptions as they were introduced to lives socially and culturally removed from their own. Regal, Eros and Metro and the films projected within them, portray society with new symbols, as they idealised Modern experience.[2]

← An advertisement in The Times of India *for the Gala Opening of the Metro, Bombay, in 1938, portraying the exterior of the cinema with its prominent corner tower designed by Thomas W. Lamb.*

The success of these cinemas was immediate and their influence long lasting. Many Indian designers adopted the Art Deco idiom, using it extensively in office and apartment blocks and, in some cases, cinema buildings. A number of architects, such as John B. Fernandes who designed the Elite, Calcutta, continued to employ what was essentially a Western decorative style. Other architects and designers, having fallen under the spell of Western Deco, started incorporating Indian features into their designs. From such a potpourri of Western and Indian imagery, comprising exaggerated flower shapes, rising suns, foliage, zigzags and circles all painted in exuberant colours and often making use of flamboyant lighting effects, emerged a new style - a fusion of Art Deco with Hindu and Mughal motifs which was given the name Indo-Deco. One of its most accomplished exponents was the designer W. M. Namjoshi, who, during a career lasting forty-odd years, was responsible for some thirty cinemas including the Liberty in Bombay, the extravagant Raj Mandir in Jaipur and, towards the end of his life, the Mangala in Pune.

From the mid-1930s onwards, cinemas were also built in a Moderne or streamlined style: characterised by round-cornered exteriors, often with a dramatic, horizontal emphasis as part of a symmetrical composition of parallel strip mouldings, rows of small windows and a canopy, contrasted with vertical accents like stairwells, pylons and fins. Before turning to a more functional modernism, the Bombay architect G. B. Mhatre designed a wealth of Moderne and Art Deco buildings in Bombay and at least one cinema, the Alankar at Bangalore. For more than thirty years, Moderne, Art Deco and its Indian variant, Indo-Deco were the dominant styles of Indian cinema architecture and were still employed occasionally as recently as the mid-1980s.

← (top left) *New Shirin, Ghorapadeo, Mumbai. The local suburban venue opened in c.1940. Nowadays, much of the colourful Art Deco façade is obscured by large posters;* (top right) *The Kamadhenu, Chennai, started in 1952.*

← (bottom left) *The Kumar, Old Delhi, opened as Sundar Talkies in 1933. The façade incorporates Art Deco and Mughal features;* (bottom right) *The entrance of Hind Mata, Dadar, Mumbai, surmounted by the figure of its namesake, Mother India. It opened in 1930.*

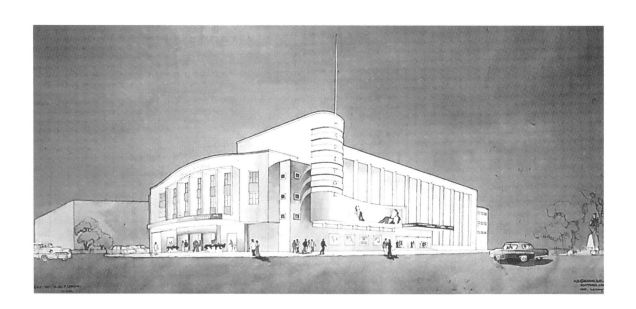

↑ *Perspective of the unexecuted scheme for the Capitol, Bombay, designed by Gregson, Batley & King in 1940.*

→ *The Orient, Kolkata, opened in the late 1940s. The interior of the 1,076-seat cinema is now clad in timber and acoustic panels, but from the little original decoration still visible an extensive Indo-Deco scheme may exist underneath.*

The Purpose-Built Cinema: Changing Styles and Fashions

The Purpose-Built Cinema: Changing Styles and Fashions

Apart from Moderne and Art Deco, architecture in India during the final decades of British Rule was influenced by the European classicism of Lutyens and Baker, the Indo-Saracenic style or a nationalistic Revivalism looking to pre-British antecedents. However, none of these was employed to any great extent in cinema buildings. As already mentioned, classicism was chosen for the first movie theatres in New Delhi and despite being widely used during an earlier period for drama theatres, it is uncommon in cinemas elsewhere. A purely Indian architectural style was rarely employed for entertainment venues, but examples of indigenous decoration are found in many cinemas. The Manprakash in Jaipur incorporates the local vernacular and Mughal arches outside and similarly styled arches and Hindu decoration inside. At the Ganga in Bikaner, Mughal decoration is found throughout what is otherwise a classical building. For the exterior of the Golcha in Jaipur, the architects Master, Sathe & Kothari created a façade with Mughal detailing in what might be termed stripped vernacular, whilst at the Golcha in New Delhi, W. M. Namjoshi included stylised temple bells in his auditorium coving. Built recently at Suraj in the State of Gujarat is the Raj Mahal, which opened in 1999; its exterior is a simplified reproduction of the famous Hawa Mahal in Jaipur, an extraordinary, five-storey building with a façade of over nine hundred small windows that enabled the ladies of the harem to view passing processions without being seen. A unique combination of the indigenous, the classical and the Indo-Saracenic fashioned and transmuted by a strongly sculptural, Art Deco inspiration is found at the Chittar Palace and its theatre cum cinema at Jodhpur designed by Henry Vaughan Lanchester between 1929 and 1944.

← A detail of the auditorium at the 1954 Golcha, New Delhi, where the designer W. M. Namjoshi incorporated stylised temple bells in the lighting coves.

4. Royal Patronage

The major developments of Indian cinema took place in cities that lay within the territories under direct British administration, but Royal Patronage also played an important role in the Princely States. The Nizam of Hyderabad, for example, flirted with both film production and cinema exhibition, but his support for the Lotus Film Company could not long co-exist with his strict Islamic beliefs. In the 19th century, the Maharajah of Jaipur built a theatre, the Ramprakash, which a later Maharajah converted into a cinema. This latter Maharajah, Man Singh, also built a new cinema, the eponymous Manprakash and financed another, the Polo Victory.

At Jodhpur, the Maharajah owned two cinemas in the city: one now demolished the other the long-closed Stadium and he incorporated a luxurious, private auditorium in his monumental new palace. Still more remarkable was the Maharajah of Bikaner, who, besides running film shows at his palace, erected a public cinema in the city and would from time to time exert the Royal Prerogative to ensure that it ran the films he wanted to see.

↑ *The Sun, a symbol of the former Princely State of Jaipur, on the exterior of the Poly Victory.*

5. Travelling and Temporary Cinemas

Cinema buildings are predominantly features of the metropolitan and urban environment, concentrated for the most part in the centre of large conurbations. In India, however, these account for only one quarter of the population, the majority live in villages and small rural communities and many are in districts far too remote for any conventional cinema to operate. Travelling cinemas provide an economically viable alternative in such places, where the opportunity of ever seeing a film projected on to a big screen would otherwise be denied.

Dating back to the days of itinerant entertainers and the lantern shows in tented cinemas, the Travelling Talkies of today are quite different - semi-permanent structures that stay put in one place for a number of years rather than just a few days. A graphic description of these cinemas was given in evidence to the 1928 Indian Cinematograph Commission:

> The lowest class of spectator has to squat on the ground and the benches and chairs in the other classes are in wretched condition and infested by bugs. There is no proper ventilation and most of the theatres are merely corrugated iron sheds.[3]

Little has changed. Sited within a secure, walled compound, a travelling cinema is rarely more than a crude shack with bamboo poles supporting a roof of corrugated sheeting; some are no more than open-sided structures covered by palm thatching. Walls, where they exist, are likely to be constructed using metals sheets or concrete blocks laid with a dry mortar set by humidity and rain.

Before opening for business, the proprietor of one of these venues must obtain a licence from the State Government for permission to erect a temporary cinema on a designated site for up to three or maybe five years. At the end of the period, the entire structure must be dismantled and removed. Once a new licence has been obtained, the cinema may set up on the new site, where the re-assembling process begins again: the whole procedure takes some three months to complete. Being of such simple construction, maintenance costs are low and unlike venues in urban areas, these cinemas are not subject to normal fire and other safety regulations.

One or two evening shows are run after nightfall. Admission prices are very low and the seats extremely crude or non-existent. Usually, free-standing chairs arranged in two classes are set out at the rear of the hall, whilst in front, low walls divide the area into two pens: the larger one for men, the smaller for women. Cinemagoers here squat on the earth floor to watch a film.

Many travelling cinemas are operating especially in the South. The number of such enterprises is uncertain as some outstay their licence period perhaps for years, but official estimates indicate around one third of the total cinemas in the country can be designated as "travelling".

Another type of travelling cinema existed during the silent era and possibly later: a train with a "Cinema Car" ran in the some parts of the country. A carriage was fitted with "a projector and all the necessary equipment" either for use as a mobile cinema or to project a film onto an external screen for open-air shows. A report in *The Times of India* in 1926 describes journeys between Bombay and Poona organised by G. I. P. Railways to show specialist documentaries.

More sophisticated temporary cinemas were established at the end of the Second World War to ameliorate the problem of excessive over-crowding at city-centre venues and, as popular films were securing such long runs, also help reduce the huge backlog of new features that were waiting to be shown. One such venue was designed in 1945 by D. G. Karanjgaokar of the Bombay practice Architectural Service for a site at Santa Cruz in the northern suburbs of Bombay. The building consisted solely of an auditorium with a shallow stage and a projection cabin. Front of house facilities were all external and the surrounding landscaped compound was used as a waiting room and also served as a car park. The cinema, seating 500 on a single floor, was a timber-framed structure under a single-pitched roof. The life span of such venues varied, but no evidence has been found that any are still extant.

→ *R.M.V. Touring Talkie, Kobalam – near the Coast Road south of Chennai. The cinema is closed awaiting an official decision on its future after outstaying its licence period.*

→ *The auditorium of the Om Sakthi, Kelam Balkkai - a small settlement south of Chennai. The screen is simply a sheet stretched across the end wall. Patrons in the two front pens squat on the earth floor to watch a film.*

6. Modernism and After

Cinema designers in India showed little interest in the Modern Movement during the 1930s and 1940s, although one cinema of the period was designed in the International Style: the Lighthouse in Calcutta is by the Dutch architect Willem M. Dudok. However, resistance to Modernism evaporated after the death of Gandhi in 1948 and, thereafter, many cinema buildings were indebted to this Western style. As Professor Vikram Bhatt explains:

> With the demise of Mahatma Gandhi – and his intransigent resistance to the lure of modern technology – and Jawaharlal Nehru's subsequent assumption of full political leadership in 1948, the way was opened up for an Indian development policy modelled on the science and industry of the West.[4]

Nehru, in his desire for a complete break with the past, with colonialism and, as he saw it, its architectural representation in the classicism of Lutyens, sought a different, modern architectural vocabulary for India, one that would epitomise the spirit of the new emerging country. He embraced not an Indian style but European Modernism and a few years later was instrumental in the appointment of Le Corbusier as principal architect for the new City of Chandigarh. Remarking on this choice, the architectural historian G. H. R. Tillotson wrote:

> Compared with anything that had been built in India, his designs...were startlingly and uncompromisingly modern......Though Le Corbusier's link with India's architectural past was at best tenuous, the future was firmly in his grip.[5]

For Indian architects, the impact of the European Master was profound. Henceforth, buildings designed by many architects of the new generation would to a greater or lesser extent reflect this aesthetic. First under his spell was the team of architects working on the

→ *The Neelam, Chandigarh, opened in 1965 - the second of three cinemas designed by Aditya Prakash for the new city. His design pays homage to the work of Le Corbusier and with its extensive use of brick, to Pierre Jeanneret - one of the principal architects of the Chandigarh Capital Project.*

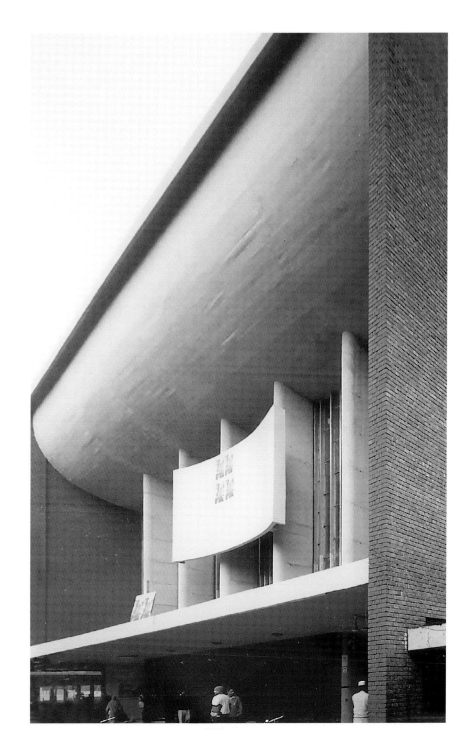

Chandigarh Capital Project responsible for design of the new city. For the next thirty years, the cinemas built in Chandigarh, all of whose architects were at some stage employed by the Capital Project, demonstrated this influence. Two of Aditya Prakash's three cinemas in the 1960s were clearly designed in homage to Le Corbusier and his cousin, Pierre Jeanneret, one of the other senior architects working on the Project. By the time the next group of cinemas was built between the mid-1970s and the early 1980s - the work of Ripudaman Singh Lall and Harbinger Singh Chopra - an austere Brutalism held sway. Subsequent venues in the region have more or less continued to adopt this latter style.

↑ Model of a cinema for New Delhi designed by Shiv Nath Prasad in the early 1960s. Of reinforced in-situ concrete with the auditorium, egg-shaped on plan, raised above front of house and parking areas - the latter an unprecedented facility in India at the time. The auditorium with 1000 seats was designed on a single rake with a projection cabin, cantilevered high above the rear stalls, equipped for Cinerama and Cinemascope. Excavation work for foundations was in progress when the owner died suddenly and the scheme was abandoned soon after.

With Modernism virtually decreed a national style, it was widely employed after Independence in the development of New Delhi not least in its cinemas. Whereas none built in the capital during the British period can lay claim to equal those in Bombay or Calcutta, from the 1960s onwards they stand pre-eminent. Throughout the latter half of the twentieth century, projects both official and private provided unprecedented opportunities for a number of major architects. Most remarkable are the Shri Ram Centre of 1966-69 by the Corbusian disciple Shiv Nath Prasad, the Chanakya by Prakash N. Mathur which opened in 1969, the Shakuntalam of 1972 by Raj Rewel and Charles Correa's new building for the British Council of 1989-92. The work of two American architects is also represented: the Sheila, which opened in 1961, is the only work in India by the influential theatre architect Ben Schlanger and two cultural complexes which include auditoria, the India International Centre of the early 1960s and the India Habitat Centre built between 1987-94 are the work of Joseph Allen Stein.

Elsewhere, other international influence can be detected. The architectural forms of Oscar Neimeyer are apparent in the sinuous compositions of Yahya C. Merchant's (demolished) Apsara of 1965 in Bombay and Srikrishna L. Chitale's Lido of 1972 in Mysore. The interiors of several cinemas in Calcutta dating from the mid-1950s suggest at least a passing acquaintance with the Festival of Britain and Scandinavian design is a probable model for the auditorium at the National Film Archive in Pune. In most cases, however, cinema architecture during the second half of the twentieth century reflected the prevailing Modernist aesthetic tempered, often somewhat perversely, by an enthusiasm for arbitrary ornamentation.

Nevertheless, even as Modernism swept nearly all before it, siren voices were raised by an older generation of Indian architects, who espoused Gandhian ideals and urged the development of an indigenous architectural tradition employing labour-intensive crafts and building methods. Whilst ignored by most, a number of younger architects took up this challenge. Although some merely applied superficial, indigenous decoration to what were essentially modernistic structures, others, whilst fully engaging modern technology, created contemporary

buildings employing traditional construction techniques. Such an aesthetic is found in the buildings of Joseph Allen Stein at the Lodi Gardens in New Delhi; still more so in the work of Uttam C. Jain, which uses steel-frame structures co-joined with labour-intensive masonry. The exteriors of his cinemas at Jodhpur and Balotra are simple and massive, fortress-like, stone structures, but embrace a surprising Post-Modern playfulness within.

From the mid-1980s onwards, a few tentative Post-Modern details appear in the designs of many new theatres; at others, especially for the new multiplexes, architects have indulged in something of a stylistic free-for-all, cheerfully mixing such disparate elements as 1930s Moderne with classical and indigenous features.

↑ *The auditorium of the Apsara, Mumbai, opened in 1965, demolished 1999. Tiny spotlights in the black ceiling suggested a starlit night sky. Wire sculptures on the side walls depicted stylised horsemen. (from an old photostat of the cinema's inaugural brochure.)*

← *(top left) Star City, Mahim, in the northern suburbs of Mumbai opened in1998 – a new up-market single-screen venue replacing an earlier cinema, the Paradise, on the same site.*

← *(top right) India Habitat Centre, Lodi Estate, New Delhi, designed by Joseph Allen Stein in 1987-94. A nine-acre development of screened courtyards with the concrete walls of the surrounding buildings clothed in 'vertical gardens'. The entrance of the 525-seater auditorium is on one side of a sunken rondel. The cinema is the home of the Habitat Film Club – the Delhi equivalent of London's National Film Theatre.*

← *Sangam, Mysore, designed by K. N. Srinivasan of Madras and Bangalore, opened in 1971. The external ramp leads to the balcony foyer. Film promotion in Mysore takes a novel form: giant cut-out images of popular stars are lashed to bamboo poles and processed ceremonially through the streets to advertise a new blockbuster. These ten-metre high figures, hand-painted at workshops in the city, are then erected against the façade of the cinema throughout the run of a film.*

7. Later Developments

The first multi-screen development in India, the Devi in Madras, opened in 1972 with one auditorium, since increased to five. Comparable venues ranging from twinned auditoria to four-screen and one or two five-screen complexes now exist; yet compared with the West, multiplexes in India are still relatively uncommon. Almost exclusively housed in new buildings and as in the West, they are, in essence, industrial sheds containing three or four cinemas with superficial decoration applied to the exterior and front of house areas. One, however, the Anupam-4 in New Delhi is a conversion financed jointly by an Australian Corporation in partnership with an local entrepreneur. It is, so far, the only four-screen complex operating in what was previously a single-screen cinema, but this venture with its dashing American styling has been an enormous success and may herald a future trend. In contrast, the newly built City Pride in Pune re-invents the elegance and style of the old movie 'dream palace'. Whilst the exterior displays a somewhat bland Post-Modernism, the interior employing expensive materials and imaginative, modern lighting effects has created a luxurious twenty-first century venue with enormous front of house spaces and four auditoria offering exceptional comfort.

Although passé in America, the drive-in cinema is relatively new to India, no doubt due in part to the low percentage of car ownership. A drive-in has been operating on the outskirts of Mumbai for many years and an up-market drive-in complex opened near seaside holiday resorts south of Chennai in 1991. With the wealthier young now able to own a car, the excitement these cinemas once generated in the West is being experienced in India today.

IMAX, the venue with the giant screen, is the latest development to arrive in the country. One of its characteristic spherical auditoria opened in the suburbs of Mumbai in Spring 2001; another four conventional cinemas within the one complex are under construction. The arrival of such large-scale, American and Australian corporate investment after an absence of nearly fifty years is likely to herald far-reaching changes in the industry.

→ *The Prarthana Beach Drive-In, East Coast Road, Injambarkham, south of Chennai.*

THE THEATRE
of Tomorrow...

LIKE a poet's Vision it calls us - the palatial picture-house! Within it, life's light and shade are reproduced with flawless effect · each tone and pitch of the world's voice realistically meet us. And before we are gripped by the drama as well as in the interval and after the show, there, are comfort and luxury in the spacious carpeted halls hung with masterpieces of painting, strewn with smooth and polished furniture, equipped with running milk-bars and food-counters that are clean, bright, quick-serviced. All needs-social and practical no less than artistic and scientific - are satisfied by the theatre awaiting us at the end of the war.

★ THE HALL THAT ENVELOPES YOU IN SPLENDOUR . . . . . .

★ THE MILK - BAR AND FOOD-COUNTER THAT TUNE YOU UP . . . .

PHOTOPHONE EQUIPMENTS LTD.

BOMBAY · CALCUTTA · LAHORE
DELHI · MADRAS · KARACHI

...LET US PLAN IT FOR YOU!

8. Buildings and Equipment

That such a huge country, stretching from the tropics in the South to the Himalayas in the North, should produce no regional variation in its cinema architecture is extraordinary. Nowhere do local building styles or climatic conditions appear to have exerted any significant influence and it is apparent that the prevailing fashions in architecture and design imported from Europe and America were of far greater importance to cinema designers. Yet in India, cinema buildings have also to contend with monsoons, in some places heavy snowfalls and be able to accommodate an audience in at least a modicum of comfort in soaring temperatures and high humidity. Externally, many are concrete-rendered over a brick structure with a corrugated sheet roof. To provide much needed shade during the hottest part of the day, entrances, where possible, face towards the North or East. Internal finishes are usually of marble, concrete or terrazzo for floors and plaster, wood panelling or marble cladding for walls creating airy and uncluttered spaces. House lights are generally extremely low and although many cinemas have decorative lighting installed, it is often no longer in working order. Some prestigious venues, though, do present elaborate displays of changing colours and patterns to entertain the audience before the show starts and during the interval. The most frequently encountered auditorium plan is a simple, rectangular hall with the seats set in straight rows; until recently, only the best houses had auditoria with splayed walls and staggered seating.

The treatment of the screen itself is an unusual feature of Indian cinemas; the use of any format-masking is extremely rare - the National Film Archive of India is one exception - and most screens are either placed within deep sloping embrasures, which are almost invariably painted white, or entirely fill one wall of an auditorium. The ragged edges of the projected picture surrounded by a frame of the unlit areas of the screen are thus visible to the audience. Why this practice should have achieved near universal acceptance in the country is unclear;

← *Photophone was established in India by RCA to provide a complete service for supplying and fitting out the technical equipment and furnishings required for a new venue or to modernise an existing one. Projection and sound equipment was manufactured under licence in the country.*

that it equates with the theories propounded by Ben Schlanger which he applied at the Shiela, New Delhi, is almost certainly coincidental. Many cinema owners suggest a far more prosaic explanation: black is perceived as an inauspicious colour that neither the exhibitor nor the audience would want to see surrounding the projected image of their favourite stars.

In older cinemas, carpets and drapes are uncommon, but occur occasionally in foyers and restaurants. However, some luxurious houses and most of the new multiplexes have carpeting in the auditoria as well. Air conditioning is provided at newer and more upmarket theatres; few extend this to front of house areas. A forest of fans suspended from the ceiling or even open roof flaps may be the only air-cooling in poorer and older theatres.

Most projection equipment is manufactured under licence inside the country. High customs duties and other restrictions act as a deterrent against imports and all but a handful of venues still operate traditional projectors; use of the platter system is exceptional. Less prosperous cinemas often have to make do with old equipment; fifty-year old projectors are commonplace and considerably older mono amplifiers are still in use in many unmodernised cabins. Even when new equipment is installed, the old system is usually retained as a back-up alongside such paraphernalia as ancient gramophones, glass-slide projectors, old valve amplifiers and *ad hoc* wiring. Frequent power cuts make a generator a necessity at every venue, however rundown. The unreliable electricity supply and fluctuating current deters many owners from investing in the best and most expensive light sources from overseas, but such equipment is installed by a few top venues in order to provide the highest quality picture available.

→ (clockwise from bottom left) *The Regal, New Delhi, uses Magnivox/Hi-Lite 130 projectors with a c.1940 Peerless Kalee in reserve (The Chief Projectionist (left) is standing next to one of our Delhi guides, Mosul Azaad.); Brenkert Enarcs, c.1950, at Radhu Talkies, Shahadra, a small local venue on the outskirts of Delhi; Gaumont Kalee (GB Model 2), installed 1943, at the Casino, Chennai; the Excelsior, Old Delhi uses Bauers, c.1960s and Klangfilm mono sound. An ancient Motograph projector is still in working order; Ashcroft Super Cinex with Bauer optics at the Shiela, New Delhi; the Shree Maruti, Mysore, has only one projector, a Bestex, c1960. Without interrupting a show, one operator swaps spools as the other first splices and then separates the ends of the reels as the film goes through the projector. It only takes a matter of seconds and practice has made the operation look remarkably simple.*

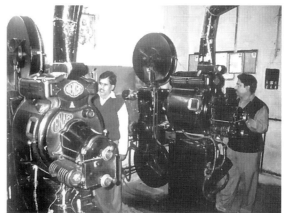

Exhibiting Movies in India

9. Exhibiting Movies in India

As a proportion of the population, India has fewer cinemas than most other countries in Asia and a considerably lower provision than in the West. Since Independence, frequent demands have been made for more outlets to accommodate the rapidly increasing population. In the 1950s and early 1960s, a programme to construct new cinemas across the country was instituted by the industry and at the same time, many older houses were completely rebuilt or refurbished with facilities upgraded for both the new Cinemascope format and stereo sound. Then, inexplicably, for a few years in the mid-1960s, the Government used every possible means to obstruct the development of more cinemas, but after a policy turn-around, which coincided with a big increase in cinema attendance, many new establishments opened in an attempt to satisfy the pent-up demand. Yet despite this, by the early 1980s, Government Ministers alarmed by continuing under-provision, were calling for an increase of over 6,000 new cinemas in a ten-year period. Plans were even mooted for the provision of State finance. Neither scheme was acted upon, changes were dictated by commercial logic: during boom years new venues opened, constructed by the industry itself; in less fortuitous times, new building ceased and a number of established theatres closed.

The film historian B. V. Dharap calculated that 420 cinemas existed in India in 1931, 1,265 in 1939, rising to around 4,000 by 1950.[6] Subsequent figures are much less precise: anything up to a four-fold increase is estimated to have occurred during the next thirty years. Since the mid-1980s, the industry has been in recession in most parts of the country and a steady decline has reduced the total to around 12,500 today nearly all of which are single screens.

In recent years, many older, city-centre cinemas have gone out of business and suburban replacements have until now been insufficient to compensate for all the closures. However, at least for the moment, the total number of venues has stopped declining and the situation is

← The festive display of posters at the entrance of the Odeon complex, Hyderabad.

1	Andhra Pradesh	2,763
2	Arunachal Pradesh	2
3	Assam	137
4	Bihar	320
5	Delhi	58
6	Gujarat	434
7	Goa, Daman and Diu	21
8	Haryana	101
9	Himachal Pradesh	15
10	Jammu and Kashmir	16
11	Karnataka	1,212
12	Kerala	1,312
13	Madhya Pradesh	443
14	Maharashtra	1,113
15	Manipur	11
16	Meghalaya	9
17	Mizoram	3
18	Nagaland	6
19	Orissa	142
20	Punjab	141
21	Rajasthan	273
22	Sikkim	2
23	Tamil Nadu	2,339
24	Tripura	7
25	Uttar Pradesh	1,045
26	West Bengal	411
27	Andaman and Nicobar Islands	1
28	Chandigarh	7
29	Dadra and Nagar Haveli	2
30	Pondicherry	41

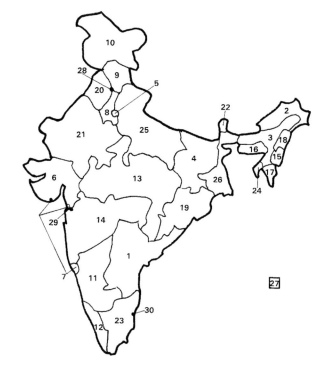

The number of cinemas, including permanent and touring venues, operating in each State or Union Territory of India in March 2000. (Information supplied by the Cinematograph Exhibitors' Association of India)

now more or less stable. In round figures, the population of India today is over one billion, which equates with a provision of one auditorium per 80,000. Britain, in contrast, with around 550 cinemas and some 2,100 screens[7] serving a population of about fifty-eight million has one auditorium for every 28,000. The deficit in India is further exacerbated by the uneven distribution: over 50% of the venues are concentrated in just four southern States. In addition, the auditoria are small: the largest, purpose-built cinemas in prominent city-centre locations have around 1,500 seats, most others considerably fewer. The capacity of older houses and suburban venues ranges from about 400 in the smallest up to about 1,000, but in many, ripped or broken seats are a common sight and the number of useable seats may be considerably lower than the official total.

Seating is strictly divided into different priced classes and in some venues a low wall across the auditorium separates the classes and prevents patrons moving to a higher-priced vacant seat. Those at the rear of the circle or balcony are the most expensive, the remaining upper level seating and rear stalls somewhat cheaper and the cheapest are the few rows nearest the screen; the low price of the last is controlled by the State Government to ensure that some seats in every cinema are affordable for all but the destitute. Admission charges range from a few rupees in country districts to well over a hundred (about £1.50) in one of the smart, new multiplexes: for the average person this is an astronomical sum putting these venues out of reach of many. With the exception of the smallest houses, staff numbers are huge by Western standards. Even small suburban cinemas employ as many as thirty or forty, whilst at prestigious, city-centre theatres the total may be as high as a hundred. Front of house staff perform their duties zealously and patrons are subjected to extraordinarily firm direction and control.

Censorship and cinema licensing were introduced in 1920 by the British administration in Bombay; Calcutta, Madras and other territories followed suit, although some prohibitions would have certainly already existed in the Princely States. Clearance both nationally and locally was a pre-requisite to receiving a certificate permitting cinema exhibition in any given territory. To accommodate preview showings before the local censor, many of the important, first-run venues were provided with small private theatres. At the most luxurious, such as the Eros and the Liberty in Bombay, glamorous social events organised by the cinema owners would include private screenings. Throughout the British era, censorship was concerned primarily with political and sectarian issues; after Independence the new Government not only retained the British rules but also tightened them considerably, especially in matters of sexual explicitness. Nowadays censorship is somewhat more relaxed, although anything markedly salacious is still restricted and some age qualifications are applied to certain categories. Mainstream commercial cinemas do not, however, provide programmes specifically for children.

The first taxes on cinema exhibition were introduced in Calcutta in 1922. In the following year, similar taxes were levied in Bombay and eventually imposed everywhere. After Independence, despite the new Government's professed enthusiastic support for the film industry, entertainment taxes were increased substantially and in 1950, as part of a nationwide protest by owners against this impost, all cinemas closed for a short time. This action and the industry's continuing protestations since have generally been unsuccessful and the levels of entertainment tax, levied partly by the National and partly by the State Government, have remained unchanged for more than fifty years. Ranging from 25% up to as high as 125% of the net seat price, the tax in some States amounts to a levy on the seat itself whether occupied or not and during periods of low ticket sales this amounts to a crippling burden on the cinema's finances. *(illustrated on page 248)* The subsequent 'neon tax' has resulted in almost all illuminated signage being dismantled, although in many cases the carcass of the display remains. Recently, the Government in the State of Gujarat has offered generous tax breaks to encourage the development of new multiplex venues; other States may follow this lead.

→ *The preview theatre at the Liberty, Mumbai, designed by W. M. Namjoshi.*

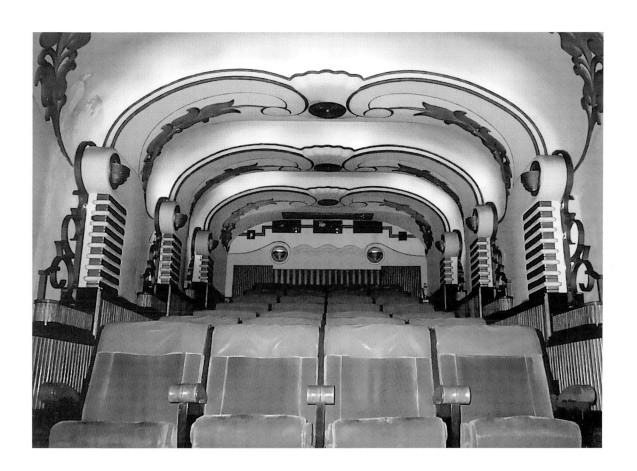

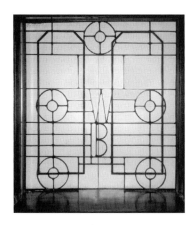

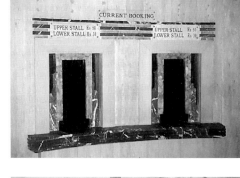

10. Going to the Pictures

Cinemas, typically, run four or five shows a day with possibly more at weekends when a different, often an old American film might be shown at a morning matinee. The practice of 'continuous performances' does not exist; neither do programmes of 'double bills' nor 'B'-films. All seats are sold for a specific show and the auditorium is completely cleared at the end of the programme. This would comprise one major feature film, which if it is an Indian production may last anything from three to three and a half hours or more accompanied by a newsreel, advertisements, often local ones on slides, and trailers for forthcoming attractions. Originally, Pathé, Movietone and Gaumont-British supplied newsreels, but in 1943 a law made the screening of an official Indian Government newsreel compulsory, a rule the Post-Independence Government retained and which continues in force today. Whether the feature film is designed to have one or not, an interval is provided in every show, when many in the audience head for large canteens and refreshment bars in the foyers or located outside in the theatre courtyard.

Seats are usually bookable in advance and when popular films sell out, a black market for tickets develops. In better-class venues, pushback seats, often luxuriously padded, are provided in the more expensive sections. *(illustrated on page 248)* This type of seat is regarded by many cinemagoers as essential when watching such long programmes. In the cheaper seats tip-ups are the norm, but in the poorest theatres, patrons may have to make do with unpadded, metal and plastic seats or, in some cases, merely a timber plank.

← Top to bottom (far left) *New Empire, Kolkata – a ticket office grille installed during the Warner Bros.' tenure; a silk canopied kiosk at the Royal Opera House, Mumbai; cylindrical, external payboxes at the (closed) Bisparupa, Kolkata.*

(middle) *Advertising a film running for more than three years at the Maratha Mandir, Mumbai; a teak and inlaid marble paybox at the Kumar, Old Delhi; an all-marble ticket office at the New Empire, Mumbai; crude pens with only tiny communication holes at Sundar Talkies, Solan, a small Himalayan town near Shimla.*

(right) *Balcony notice with a patriotic display for Republic Day at the Alexandra, Mumbai; decorative brass ticket office grille in a marble surround at the Imperial, Mumbai; a paybox at Kama Talkies, Hyderabad, which closed in 1994.*

A characteristic of Indian cinemas in the past was the practice of purdah or segregation of female patrons, who would use separate zenana entrances and sit in specially designated, screened sections of the auditorium. Purdah, a derivation from the Persian "parda", literally means a curtain and came to India with the Mughals, but was subsequently adopted by many Hindu Princes. It once led to a tragedy in a Hyderabad cinema. A member of the Official Enquiry later recorded the event:

> In (some) Indian cinemas the balcony was reserved for women and children, who viewed the film through a veil curtain while men sat below. In 1941, a disastrous fire broke out in one of these cinemas. So great was the inhibition amongst the women against being seen in public that many were burnt to death rather than face the "shame" of escaping with the crowd. The Commission of Enquiry set up afterwards....had to interview several purdah lady survivors for evidence: the examination had to be conducted through curtains.[8]

As late as the 1940s, many cinemas were still provided with purdah curtains and entrances. The coming of Independence to India and the rise of feminism led to the disappearance of segregation, but today it is still rare to see lone females in a cinema audience and unescorted women are usually seated in the balcony rather than the stalls.

Silent films were probably sufficiently understood from their images alone, but as many as four sets of intertitles were often put on a single print. Some cinemas employed an official reader to proclaim these texts for the benefit of those who could not read them. Such procedures were necessary in India because audiences might speak any of the country's fifteen recognised major languages or seven hundred-odd other languages and dialects. Cinemas either showed films in one or more of the Indian languages or presented English-language

← *An advertisement for a popular fan magazine,* The Motion Picture Magazine, *published in India during the 1930s and 1940s.*

programmes; few ran both. In all probability, Europeans rarely visited cinemas showing Indian films, whereas Indians flocked to see British and American productions. During the silent era, the majority of films shown in India came from either France or America but once sound arrived, French films could no longer compete and most city venues then concentrated on showing English-language films. Several signed up with one or other of the big Hollywood Studios, in some instances accepting an exclusive deal to show the films of that particular studio or their local distributor; thus, a cinema might become, for example, "The Home of Paramount Pictures".

At the same time, demand amongst Indian audiences for home-produced feature films increased in line with their technical and storytelling sophistication, but the innumerable Indian languages have proved an obstacle to distribution and the development of a truly national industry despite dubbing having long since replaced subtitles. Nowadays, big productions are released simultaneously in several different language versions, yet despite this, the popular appeal of many superstars remains strictly regional. In practice, production at the three major film centres and to a lesser extent distribution and exhibition is still separated by language. 'Bollywood' in Mumbai makes Hindi films distributed nationwide and to the Indian Diaspora, 'Tollywood' in Kolkata makes mostly Bengali films and 'Collywood' in Chennai produces Tamil and Telugu films which are widely shown in the south of the country and overseas. Recently, the rapidly expanding Film City at Hyderabad has begun to break down these barriers by attracting film-makers from further afield; even so, most of its productions are in the local language, Telugu. The output from studios in other States is relatively small, usually in the local language and with a restricted, regional distribution.

Most cinemas now show only Indian films. Some city-centre theatres specialise in Hollywood films or, occasionally, even a British production dubbed into Hindi; a few still present these films undubbed and as English remains the common language amongst the educated classes, they manage to find an audience. With the exception of cinemas in areas with large communities from one particular country such as the Nepalese living near Radhu Talkies on the outskirts of New Delhi, films from elsewhere are restricted to film clubs.

The commercial application of 16mm films started in India during the British time as a means of presenting films that in normal circumstances would not receive a showing in a commercial cinema. Screenings were set up in any suitable hall or auditorium; in Simla, for example, the Gaiety Theatre was appropriated for just such use, as was Viceregal Lodge for private shows. More-widespread use was made of the format for documentaries, educational films and most importantly children's film shows. Realising an enormous, potential market existed in India, MGM established a special 16mm distribution unit in the country in 1946 mainly to supply travelling and rural theatres.

The Post-Independence Government appreciated the scope offered by the smaller format and was eager to promote its installation where full 35mm facilities would prove impractical or simply too expensive. In particular, cost was a major factor inhibiting the presentation of films made specifically for children. To help overcome this problem, in 1955 the Indian Children's Film Society was established to encourage and, with outside sponsorship, finance the production and distribution of mostly 16mm films. Many eminent actors, directors and producers worked with this organisation including Ashok Kumar, Satyan Bose and Satyajit Ray, who made two adventure stories, *Sonar Kella* (1975) and *Jai Baba Felunath* (1978). Regular shows were organised in schools and community centres and under the auspices of municipal and welfare authorities, mobile cinemas were set up in the slum areas of some big cities and in remote country districts.

The original applications of 16mm film have now generally been overtaken by the widespread availability of television and video, but new uses have arisen in the case of specialist archive and art house presentations.

11. Music in the Cinema

From the start, as evidenced by the Lumière screenings at the Novelty Theatre in Bombay, film shows in India were accompanied by music. Before sound arrived, music for European and American films was usually provided by a piano or harmonium possibly with a violin accompaniment or, in larger houses, a small band of four or five musicians playing a background melody of popular tunes related as far as possible to the action appearing on screen. For indigenous films, a harmonium might also be used, but usually the accompaniment was performed by a small group playing percussion instruments like the tabla or mrudanga, a stringed tambura and possibly a flute. The music was not written down but improvised from folk tunes; in mythological stories the musicians would select instruments associated with the particular Gods portrayed. The film composer Bhaskar Chandavarkar recalled the early days:

> The harmonium and the tabla players were expected to use not only their instruments, but (also) their feet to stamp, their voices to shout and generally boost excitement during fight sequences. "Maro!", "Chup Saale!" and "Khamosh!" were words the musicians bellowed as the villain was being beaten black and blue. The musicians were in effect the first dialogue writers and dubbers; in any case they were the first commentary reader-speakers that the industry knew. [9]

Large numbers of harmoniums were exported to India from Britain and possibly other European countries, some with special adaptations such as pegged keys to enable them to function in the Indian climate. Notwithstanding the known widespread use of the instrument in both religious and entertainment establishments, no extant instrument has been located by our researches either in, or removed from, a cinema.

Little more is known about the makes, numbers or locations of any theatre organs imported into the country. One instrument, however, is recorded: a 2-manual, 8-rank Wurlitzer organ was installed in 1928 at a cost of 65,000 rupees at a Madan theatre, possibly the Elphinstone

Picture Palace in Calcutta.[10] The current whereabouts of this instrument is unknown, but reminiscing about his early cinemagoing experiences in Calcutta, the film director Satyajit Ray recalled:

> The cinema that we loved to go to then was the Madan, where the mellifluous tones of the Wurlitzer organ drowned the noise of the projector while heightening the drama on the screen.[11]

Intriguingly, in several large 1930s cinemas, decorative grille-faced chambers are placed either side of the proscenium, but confirmation of any theatre organ installation has yet to be found.

Music is an important element in Indian theatre and the extensive sequences of song and dance in most contemporary Indian films probably evolved from this tradition. In 'Bollywood' films, the musical talent is usually given equal or more prominent billing than the stars and director and music plays a major role in both the film and its promotion. Sales of sound tracks are hugely important in advertising a production and, in consequence, patrons want to hear a comparable sound quality when they visit the cinema. To satisfy these expectations, many exhibitors have afforded priority to high-quality sound systems over projection equipment. At some older venues, the ironic situation occurs of a brand new Dolby or comparable sound system installed alongside aged projectors. In addition, this necessity for high-quality sound has been responsible for ruining numerous fine interiors. To improve the acoustical characteristics of the auditorium, crude cladding, installed with little regard for any existing features, has obscured or in some cases resulted in the complete destruction or removal of the original decorative scheme. The New Empire in Kolkata, the Regal in Mumbai and the Rivoli in New Delhi are notable examples where this has occurred.

12. Current Trends

Indian film producers, in a mood of growing self-confidence following Independence, released an increasing number of films year by year. At the end of the 1980s, the total reached over nine hundred; it has since dropped back to around six hundred and fifty. For twenty-five years from 1960 to 1985, the industry expanded with one box-office success following another. Some films were so popular that venues were able to run the same feature to packed houses for many months or even several years before any fall off at the box office. However, since the boom ended in the mid-1980s, the industry has faced declining ticket sales followed by recession and contraction.

Exhibitors have generally laid the blame for this state of affairs on both a lack of original, top-class product from the studios and, more particularly, television. As a mass medium available countrywide, TV came late to India, but its subsequent popularity has had a deleterious effect on the cinema industry. Following test transmissions around Delhi in 1952, coverage slowly extended across the country; colour arrived in 1982. The decision to separate television from the State-run All-India Radio and the opening up of channels to commercial operators in 1986 led to a four-fold increase in set ownership within two years, The licensing of videos in 1989 and, more recently, the introduction of cable television increased demand still further. Access to television is now near universal in most parts of the country even if only on a communal basis in some rural settlements. Besides major cable operators like Star TV and Zee, a proliferation of channels has resulted in an endless supply of new and old feature films twenty-four hours a day, many viewable unofficially without paid subscription. Most damaging to the exhibitors is the practice of transmitting pirated prints of new feature films on or even before their theatrical release date, leaving cinemas struggling to find an audience and as a result box-office takings have sometimes shown a serious decline.

← Diana, Tardeo Junction, Mumbai – closed in the early 1990s. Barred and semi-derelict, the rendered and faience-clad exterior is rapidly deteriorating but the monogram 'D.T.' for Diana Theatre is still just visible in the centre of the façade. Tardeo junction is becoming a fashionable residential district and the cinema will probably be demolished to make way for an apartment block.

The impact of television and video, however, should be kept in perspective. Every day in India over twenty million people go to the cinema; in a single year some seven billion cinema admission tickets are sold: evidence, furthermore, of cinema admissions not at their peak but after some fifteen years of decline. In numerical terms alone, the Indian cinema industry is astonishing and like no other; proof that despite the competition from home entertainment, audiences are still willing to purchase a ticket to see a feature film projected on to a big screen. Cinemagoers are attracted in vast numbers by such popular, family-friendly films as Soojah Barjatya's *Hum Aapke Hain Kaun (What Are You To Me?)* (1994), which broke all previous Indian box-office records, and Hollywood blockbusters like *Titanic*: nonetheless, big successes like these are now increasingly rare.

↑ *The weekly seat availability notice showing a run of full houses is displayed outside the box-office of the Devi Multiplex, Chennai.*

Over the last century, the Indian film industry has altered out of all recognition. Started by enterprising individuals or members of a single family, in the years before Independence some joined forces and established dominant positions as cinema exhibitors and others ventured into film production. Similarly, a number of production companies opened cinema outlets. Family-based enterprises such as Madan Theatres Ltd, the Modi family's Western Indian Cinemas Ltd and Sidhwa and Kooka's Globe Theatres Ltd owned or operated more than one hundred cinemas apiece throughout the Sub-Continent in addition to running vast distribution agencies. These empires have either shrunk or, in the case of Madan, folded.

National exhibitor chains all but disappeared after Independence. A few businesses control fifty or so regionally-based venues, but ownership is generally a small-scale affair of a few cinemas in one locality. Nowadays, many are one-off investments made by family-owned concerns, for which the cinema is largely a minor financial, but socially prominent, activity. Whether for reasons of family pride, local status or for tax advantages, most appear unlikely to divest these assets despite their poor return or even possibly operating at a loss over many years.

Some cinemas showing films today date from the earliest years of film exhibition and examples from every subsequent period still survive: a reflection of the changes in popular entertainment fashions and architectural styles over the last century. But for reasons both economic and stylistic, entertainment venues are constantly forced to change and adapt to current trends. The question, so far unanswered, is whether the new style, luxuriously-furnished multiplexes with their state-of-the-art equipment will be any match for the architectural élan and showmanship displayed during the first one hundred years of cinema exhibition in India.

Part Two

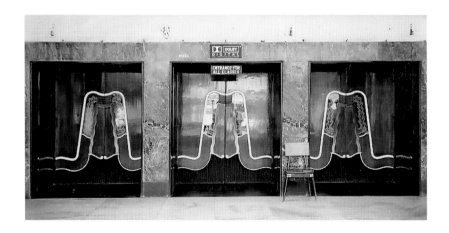

↑ *The Maratha Mandir, Mumbai, was designed by W. M. Namjoshi and opened in 1958. The entrance doors are typical of Namjoshi's sinuous designs, here incorporating teak, metalwork and engraved coloured glass.*

13. Mumbai/Bombay

European colonists first landed here in the early 16th century and in 1661 the settlement passed into British hands. What began as a group of islands surrounded by swamps has become, after extensive land reclamation, a long tapering isthmus connected to the mainland at the northern end and has developed into the richest of Indian cities with some sixteen million inhabitants. The city was called Bombay during the British era, its name changed to Mumbai in 1995 and is now the capital of Maharashtra State.

From the mid-19th century onwards, commercial success led to rapid expansion and furnished the city with an outstanding array of buildings, which fall generally into three groups: Gothic Revival, Indo-Saracenic and Art Deco.

Mumbai is today a booming financial and industrial metropolis with the sprawling film production complex of 'Bollywood' in the northern suburbs. The story of Indian cinema started in this city and for most of the last century Bombay was dominant in both film production and exhibition. Around one hundred and forty cinemas are operating within the Greater Mumbai conurbation, including some of the finest Art Deco movie palaces in the country

Watson's Hotel
Mahatma Ghandi Road

On 7th July 1896, Maurice Sestier, an emissary from the Lumière brothers of Paris, presented the first demonstration in India of projected moving pictures at a makeshift cinema set up in Watson's Hotel. Sestier had been sent out by the Lumières to promote their moving film equipment, the 'Cinématographe', in Australia, but stopped off *en route* in Bombay, where he set about promoting the new apparatus.

Precisely where the temporary cinema was established in the hotel is not documented, but it may well have been in the central, glass-roofed atrium that at one time was used for theatrical performances. The advertisements in *The Times of India* announced the arrival of the "Marvel of the Century" listing a selection of the items to be screened which included *Arrival of the Train, The Sea Bath* and *Ladies and Soldiers on Wheels. (illustrated on page 15)* The shows continued at Watson's Hotel until 15th August 1896, but the enthusiasm of the crowds was such that after the first week additional screenings were arranged at the much larger Novelty Theatre.

Watson's Hotel opened in 1869 as the Esplanade Hotel. Designed by Rowland Mason Ordish (1824-1886), apart from its cinematic significance, the building has an equally important claim to fame as the first in Bombay constructed using a prefabricated iron frame with brick infilling. The iron structure is partially visible in the pillars of the street level arcades and the old hotel lobby.

After the hotel closed the building was converted to offices and renamed Mahendra Mansions. The atrium is now disused and filled with rubble; only a few of its original decorative floor tiles remain to suggest what might have been, but a plaque unveiled on the façade in 1996 commemorates the role this building played in the arrival of cinema in India.

← *Watson's Hotel (from a print issued in c.1900).*

Gulshan Talkies

Patthe Bapurao

Throughout the latter half of the nineteenth century and first few decades of the twentieth, numerous theatres were operating in the area around Falkland Road, the former name of Patthe Bapurao, and nearby Grant Road making it the most important centre in the city for both indigenous and European-style drama.

Long before the British left, however, Falkland Road had become Mumbai's main 'red-light district' and the bad reputation of the area has hastened the decline of its legitimate entertainment venues. Nowadays, none survive as theatres, but a few original buildings still exist, albeit much altered, converted into cinemas. Charging very low prices, some attract good houses by screening violent and sexy films for the many, local unemployed males.

One such is Gulshan Talkies, the oldest venue still operating in Mumbai and probably anywhere in India. It was built by Jagannath Shankarseth and opened in 1853 as the incongruously named Grant Road Theatre. Under the patronage of the Governor of Bombay, Sir Bartle Frere, Augusto Cagli's Italian Opera Company gave performances here in the 1860s of Verdi, Rossini and Donizetti.

It is believed to have been converted into a cinema in the 1920s and during a subsequent makeover in the 1960s, a crude concrete slab superstructure was installed completely obscuring the original façade. Inside, little decoration is apparent: the interior moulded plasterwork has been either 'simplified' or brightened up with inappropriate, painted dots and amoebic shapes typical of the period. The entrance opens into a long lobby, which was originally built as an open courtyard, and leads directly into the 725-seater auditorium. X-rated films are run throughout the day, the first show commencing at 8.00am.

A few doors away stood the recently demolished Victoria Theatre, which had been converted into a cinema called Taj Talkies; a similar fate befell Nishat Talkies, the former Coronation Theatre and Daulat Talkies, previously the Baliwala Grant Theatre. Opposite, New Roshan Talkies survives and despite later crude additions the original mixture of muscular Gothic and classical details is still apparent. Moti Talkies is nearby in S.V.P. Road. Originally known as the American Joosab Cinema named after its founder, the first change was to National Cinema and after Independence to the current one. Half hidden in a high-walled compound, the building retains some classical details despite a 1962 modernisation,

↑ *The grim 1960s street frontage of Gulshan Talkies.*

Alfred Talkies

Patthe Bapurao

When it opened in the late 19th century as the Ripon Theatre, this was one of the first venues in Bombay regularly producing drama in the local dialects of Urdu, Marathi, Gujurati and Konkani. It was modernised and converted into a cinema in 1925, re-opening as the Alfred, later changed to Alfred Talkies.

The facade of stone pilasters, mouldings and perforated cornice is partly obscured by a film poster although the prominent vertical sign is still visible. The large square lobby continues in a similar style and nowadays is used for waiting. It leads directly to the stalls or up stairways embellished with richly carved newel posts to side verandahs providing access to the circle.

The auditorium layout is little changed, nevertheless, much of the original decoration is lost, simplified or obscured and the orchestra pit is boarded over. A Cinemascope screen is placed far upstage behind the flat-topped proscenium arch of moulded plaster. Concrete rendering covers the deeply curved circle front; some sections of railings have been removed and flat screeded areas at the sides fill what were once private boxes. All 938 seats have plain, unpainted metal backs; only those in the front circle have padded seats, elsewhere patrons must also make do with a metal seat.

← *The exterior of Alfred Talkies.*

→ *The auditorium with the Cinemascope screen set up inside the proscenium at the rear of the old stage.*

Edward Theatre

Kalbadevi Road

The Edward Theatre was built in 1860 as a drama theatre and still visible are the remnants of an orchestra pit, the fly tower & dressing rooms. From the street, an elaborate pedimented gateway leads to a courtyard with the auditorium in a separate building at the rear and a small office to one side. The auditorium hall, set at an angle to the street frontage, is a tall, well-mannered building in vaguely classical style. Cement-rendered walls are painted white, with a pantiled roof topped by an hexagonal cupola surmounted by a ball.

Madan Theatres Ltd. of Calcutta acquired a lease on the theatre in 1926 and converted it into a full-time cinema. Later, one of their local agents, a Parsee businessman, Bejan Dadiba Bharucha (1903-1984) joined forces with Manchersha B. Bilimoria, a supplier of film equipment in Bombay, to form the partnership of Bharucha & Bilimoria. After the collapse of the Madan chain, they took over the Edward Theatre in 1932 and to signify the installation of sound equipment, the name was changed to Edward Talkies, sometime later reverting to the original.

Throughout the 1930s, Bharucha & Bilimoria expanded rapidly, every year opening or acquiring more cinemas in different parts of the country and in 1938 taking control of All-India Theatres Sindicate Ltd., a chain operating in the State of Gurjarat. In the same year, Bharucha was elected Hon. Secretary of the Motion Picture Society of India and amongst his other duties was the editorship of *The Indian Cinematograph Year Book*.

After Bharucha's death, his widow, Gertrude, undertook an extensive restoration of the building. The original layout of proscenium, stage, stalls, deeply curved circle and balcony remained; only the stage boxes and 'gods' were closed, but not removed. The work involved new rendering on the walls and extensive repairs to the decorative plasterwork, including the attractive classical mouldings around the proscenium and the frieze on the boxes, circle and balcony fronts.

When opened, the cinema seated 828, since reduced to 509 all wooden tip-ups. Although situated in the centre of the city near several other major cinemas, the Edward is a lowly-priced, second-run house in a quiet side street.

↑ *A view of the restored auditorium from the 'gods'.*

↑↑ *Bejan Dadiba Bharucha (photographed c.1935).*

→ *The Edward Theatre at sunset. The pedimented entrance leads to the auditorium in the tall building at the rear of the courtyard.*

Capitol

Opposite Chatrapati Shivaji Terminus

The Capitol cinema was originally called the Gaiety Theatre, which opened on 6th December 1879. Situated at a busy road junction opposite two of the city's outstanding buildings, the Victoria Terminus (now Chatrapati Shivaji) and the Municipal Building, both of which are near contemporaries. Although the architect is not known, the theatre was the brainchild of the Parsee showman Kuverji Sorabji Nazir.

As a live theatre, the Gaiety produced English, Marathi and Gujarati drama, although a few film shows were presented as early as January 1897. These included items produced by Stewart's 'Vitagraph' process and later, on a return visit during the 1901 Christmas season, a programme of three short films presented *Life of Christ,* and two contemporary newsreel items, *The Queen's Funeral Procession* and *The Assassination of President McKinley.*

One notable Gaiety manager was a Bombay photographer, Harischandra Sakharam Bhatvadekar. Inspired by the Lumieres' presentation in 1896, Bhatvadekar imported a motion picture camera from Britain and is credited with being one of the first Indians to produce a moving picture film. In 1901, he shot what is referred to as (India's) "first newsreel" - the homecoming of a successful student from Cambridge. Two years later, he recorded the splendour of the King-Emperor's 1903 Durbar at Delhi. The huge success of this film led to Bhatvadekar being offered the position of Manager of the Gaiety, a post he held long after he had ceased making pictures.

In the late 1920s, the lease of the Gaiety was transferred to Globe Theatres of Calcutta, a nationwide exhibition and distribution chain. The new owners renamed the theatre the Capitol and converted it into a full-time cinema. Little structural change was necessary apart from the

↑ *An advertisement in* The Times of India *in 1927 announcing the forthcoming opening of the re-named Capitol cinema.*

→ (top) *The exterior in 2001.*

removal of a few boxes and the orchestra pit. Pay boxes with Art Deco metal grilles were installed in the lobby. The official opening took place on 20th January 1928 before a celebrity audience including the Governor of Bombay, Sir Orme Wilson.

The symmetrical facade has a triple-arched, central entrance, flanked by shops at street level and above, grouped square and round-topped windows. Originally the roof had steep mansards and pediments *(illustrated on page 21)*, which have since been removed. The 880-seat auditorium is arranged as stalls, a horseshoe-shaped circle supported by square pillars with bow-fronted boxes at the sides and a narrow gallery above. Most of the original classical decoration has been retained, including marble floors, panelled teak doors, pilasters, railings and grilles. An air extractor in the centre of a large shallow dome is surrounded by bold geometric decoration. When the proscenium was widened to accommodate the Cinemascope screen, it lost most of the surrounding mouldings but draw curtains are still used. The projection cabin was upgraded in 1999 with two Christie AutoWind-3s and two Xenon-II projectors.

In 1940, it was proposed to demolish this building and erect a new cinema in Art Deco style, but the scheme came to nothing. *(illustrated on page 32)* The architects were the Bombay firm of Gregson, Batley & King, responsible for many other buildings in the city including the Central Railway Station of 1930.

↓ *The auditorium*

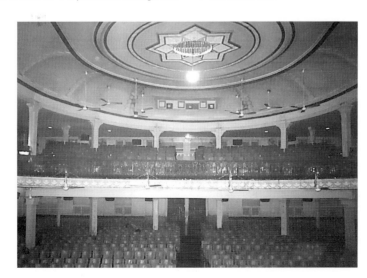

New Excelsior

Amarti Keshav Marg, Fort

The New Excelsior stands on the site of a demolished late 19th-century theatre, the Novelty, a three-storey building in a heavy Italianate style. It was the home of Batliwalla's famous Parsee repertory group, the Victoria Theatre Company, and the contemporary English-language newspapers referred to it as 'a local house' presumably to indicate one not patronised by the British.

As soon as it was realised how popular the Lumières' 'Cinématographe' presentations were at Watson's Hotel, extra shows were arranged at this theatre. *(illustrated on page 16)* The screenings started on 14th July in tandem with those at Watson's, but continued for several weeks "well into the monsoon season" after those at the Hotel stopped. The programmes, initially comprising twelve short films, were increased to include as many as twenty-four accompanied by music under the direction of F. Seymour Dove, the organist at the Bombay church of St. John's, Colaba. Within a couple of weeks, a notice was advertising "Reserved Boxes for Purdah Ladies and their Families" and the theatre had introduced a scale of prices reflecting the position and distance of the seat from the screen.

When the Lumière programmes finished, the theatre reverted to live entertainment, although around the turn of the century cinema shows were presented occasionally by a group of Europeans working in Bombay for the Paris-India Motor Car Company. A few years later, two Italians involved in tent-show film exhibition, Colonello and Cornaglia, using films and projection equipment supplied by Pathé's newly opened Bombay office, leased the theatre, founding Excelsior Cinematograph in c.1907. A year later, a syndicate headed by Khan Bahadur Ardeshir Billimoria took control of this and the nearby Empire Theatre before merging these interests with Madan Theatres Ltd. For several years, the theatre was referred to as either the Novelty or the Excelsior, its advertising confusingly including both names, but eventually the Excelsior name stuck and the former title dropped completely.

In 1911, a newsreel of the F.A. Cup Final was

screened in a programme with *The Dancer of Siva*, a coloured film with a story based on Hindu legends. *(Illustrated on page 16)* Later the same year, the 'Auxetophonoscope', a pioneering system for marrying moving pictures with sound, was presented at the theatre. These shows included selections from popular operas, *The Merry Widow, Carmen* and *La Boheme*. However, stage shows continued to predominate, helping to secure its reputation as an important venue in Bombay for sophisticated entertainment. Pavlova, Heifetz, Galli-Curci, Clara Butt and Harry Lauder were some of the major international artists who appeared.

When Madan Theatres relinquished possession, it was acquired by the Modi family's Western India Cinemas Ltd. and the policy of mixed programming was continued into the 1960s, a Scandinavian Ice Revue being one of the last. Despite many changes of ownership, the Excelsior, with much of its original theatrical layout and décor intact, survived until the early 1970s, when the theatre was closed and the entire site cleared for redevelopment.

Bombay architects N. N. Mehtia and L. M. Contractor designed a new multi-purpose structure, which opened in 1974. As originally planned, the building comprised a cinema - the New Excelsior - occupying the entire basement, ground and first floor areas with, to one side, an eight-storey office tower rising from the second floor level. Building regulations at the time did not permit any other structure immediately above a public auditorium, but after this stipulation was relaxed, further office accommodation was built on top of the auditorium and a new facade added. Interior decoration in the cinema was the work of W. M. Namjoshi. The large open-plan foyer is expensively finished in pink marble with polished granite

columns. Walls are faced with glass panels containing colourful pictures illustrating folk tales; one shows a golden-haired mermaid on a shimmering sea. The ceiling in the auditorium is tinted silver, indirectly illuminated and a broad pale blue and silver moulded feature runs longitudinally finishing above the screen in a fan shape. Abstract-patterned panels on the walls are painted in subtle shades of brown and buff. The small stage is without a proscenium, but a curtain and narrow pelmet is suspended in front of the floating 'Dimension - 150' screen echoing its deep curve. The 1,101 padded pushback seats are on a stepped, single floor.

↑ *The New Excelsior with the office tower built over the auditorium.*

↑↑ *An advertisement in* The Times of India *of 1911 announcing the 'Auxetophonoscope' - an early sound and picture system.*

← *The Novelty Theatre (photographed in c.1905).*

Alexandra
Bellasis Road

Entry is through a canopied gateway leading to a narrow courtyard. The auditorium, seating 527, is set back from the roadway surrounded by open verandahs behind square columns at both stalls and balcony level with access to the upper level by an external staircase. *(illustrated on page 58)* Classical decoration is present on the exterior walls and around the auditorium doors, but none visible inside, which has been clad in acoustic tiles and its original design is no longer apparent.

Despite its present unprepossessing appearance, the Alexandra has important historical links with the early days of Indian Cinema. The first Alexandra Theatre, of uncertain date and probably built as a drama theatre, was already operating as a part-time cinema when acquired in 1914 by the newly-formed partnership of Abdulally Esoofally (1884-1957) and Ardeshir Marwan Irani (1886-1969). After some seven years, the partnership built the present venue, which opened in October 1921 as the Alexandra Cinema; its first presentation was the Sam Goldwyn production *Woman and the Puppet* starring Geraldine Farrar.

Esoofally and Irani were important pioneers in the Indian film industry. From about 1908, Esoofally was travelling in many countries of the Far East, exhibiting films in a portable tented cinema. Meanwhile, Irani, who had studied at the J. J. School of Art in Bombay, began by distributing foreign films in India and, in due course, Carl Laemmle, Head of Universal Pictures in Hollywood, appointed him as the local representative. After merging their businesses in 1914, the Esoofally-Irani Partnership continued for some fifty-five years, although Irani soon branched out into production and direction, enthused, so he reminisced some thirty years later, by the early films of the Indian director Dada Saheb Phalke. In 1920, he launched the first of several, short-lived production companies and in 1926, together with Esoofally and others, started the Imperial Film Company. This studio produced the first Indian sound feature film, *Alam Ara*, which Irani also directed. It was premiered on the 14th March 1931 at the Partnership's Cinema Majestic at Girgaum, Bombay (demolished). Irani is credited with making about two hundred and fifty films, including India's first indigenous colour film, *Kisan Kanya* (1937), in the Cinecolour process. Imperial Films ceased trading in 1938 but Irani remained active in the industry and his Jyoti Studio, formed in 1939, was handed on to his son. In 1974, Bombay's Kennedy Bridge was renamed Ardeshir Bridge in his honour.

← (top left) *Abdulally Esoofally and Ardeshir Marwan Irani. (from an old photostat of a brochure celebrating Imperial Films, c.1951)*

← *The Alexandra. The paybox is situated under the gabled entrance. The auditorium is housed in a separate building away from the road at the rear of a walled courtyard.*

← *A poster for Irani's Alam Ara – the first sound feature film produced in India.*

New Empire
Marzaben Road, Fort

In 1908, the *Bombay Gazette* reported that it "was difficult to recall a time when plans for a real English theatre (for Bombay) were not in the air". After many abortive schemes including a previous one for this site, eventually, on the 15th June 1906 the City of Bombay Building Company started work on a new theatre, the Empire. According to the newspaper, the architect was Arthur Payne with interior design undertaken by the local firm O'Connor & Gerald. The theatre opened on 21st February 1908 with an evening of varied entertainment performed by Batliwalla's Victoria Company.

↑ *The original exterior (photographed in 1946).*

↑↑ *Kekhasru Modi and guests assembled in the foyer for the Gala Opening of the remodelled cinema in 1948.*

→ *The new exterior of the New Empire (photographed in 1948)*

The substantial building, in Baroque style with a prominent corner pediment, immediately established itself as one of the most lavish and up to date in the East, offering full stage facilities, a large orchestra pit, the latest lighting equipment and what was described as a unique (in Asia) pink silk drop curtain. Under a domed ceiling, the auditorium of approximately 1,000 seats comprised stalls, boxes, circle and gallery and was reputedly the first theatre in Asia to use a cantilevered construction.

Precisely when films started being shown here is not known, but in 1920 the second part of the D. W. Griffith epic *Intolerance* was presented at the theatre and throughout the decade, drama seasons were interspersed with film shows. By the 1930s, it had become a full-time cinema but the existing theatrical layout and facilities were retained. Under the subsequent ownership of the Modi family circuit, Western India Cinemas Ltd., its name was changed to New Empire in 1937.

This enterprise had started in 1915, when three Parsee bothers, Sohrab, Rustom and Kekhasru Modi, who operated a travelling cinema in Gwalior, opened their first permanent venue at Deolali. Sohrab soon left the business, becoming a famous stage actor specialising in interpretations of Shakespeare in Hindi and subsequently a successful film director. Rustom joined him in 1935 to set up their own production company, the Stage Film Company and a year later with Abdeali Musaji started Minerva Movietone, which developed into one of India's major film companies. Kekhasru remained a film exhibitor, building up a huge circuit at one time controlling over one hundred and thirty cinemas throughout India, now reduced to three - the Elite in Kolkata, the West End in Pune and this one.

After Independence, the cinema was extensively re-modelled under the supervision of the British architect M. A. Riddley Abbott. It re-opened in 1948, in a stylish Art Deco guise, with a Gala Performance of Otto Preminger's film *Forever Amber* starring Linda Darnell and Cornell Wilde. The new decorative scheme had swept away all traces of the original Baroque design. The exterior now presents an elegant, rendered facade with shallow mouldings and panels picked out in shades of grey and red, a prominent illuminated canopy and a vertical sign at one corner. Recently, a railed security courtyard has been created in front of the building.

It is uncertain who was responsible for the interior, although a number of designers working in Bombay at the time – Karl Schara, Fritz von Drieberg and W. M. Namjoshi – have, at various times, been credited with the work. The restrained styling of the exterior is continued in the drum-shaped lobby, housing pay boxes faced with different coloured marbles. *(illustrated on page 58)* The foyers and passages have more exuberant decor; in particular, coved circles and swirling strips in the ceilings with recessed lighting and teak doors embellished with wavy aluminium or brass strips, a feature used throughout the building. The cinema seats 983 in the stalls and circle; the projection cabin now occupies part of the old balcony. The auditorium is relatively plain, but made magical by the subtle use of recessed lighting in various shades of yellow and orange. This illuminates the overlapping panels along the walls, the covings in the ceiling and under the circle and reaches a thrilling climax around the proscenium, where the colours either highlight or silhouette reeded columns and moulded decoration. The painted surfaces are in muted colours reinstating those of the original scheme and the pink silk drop curtain has been restored. In the projection box are three Ashcroft/Century projectors and a stereo sound system. To one side is the old gramophone room, which formerly provided interval music.

By the early 1990s, this cinema had become rather rundown, but in 1996, an extensive restoration programme was planned by local architects under the guiding hand of the owner, Roosi K. Modi, the son of Kekhasru. The cinema has been returned to its former glory and is one of the finest Art Deco interiors in Mumbai.

↑ *At night, looking into the entrance underneath the illuminated canopy.*

→ *A detail of the decoration in the auditorium.*

↓ *The illuminated proscenium.*

Royal Opera House

Mama Parmanand Marg, Malabar Hill

The Royal Opera House was conceived in 1908 by its owner Jahankir Fardonzi Karaka, a wealthy Bombay businessman, in partnership with the Calcutta-based theatrical entrepreneur and manager Maurice Bandman, as a new luxurious venue for musical and theatrical productions. The foundation stone was laid in 1910. Karaka was the driving force behind the enterprise and reputedly had a hand in its design. The architect has yet to be identified.

The huge Baroque structure is constructed of Porbundar sandstone and brick. A palatial front elevation with deeply moulded pilasters, window and door embrasures and cast-iron balustrades below a carved pediment depicting musicians and instruments, is surmounted by a heroic sculptural group of four figures, the smaller pair supporting an heraldic shield. Originally, a tall, canopied tower was at one end, later this was lowered and now balances the shorter one on the opposite corner. Entry is through any one of seven, round-headed doorways in the facade. One side elevation faces upon a large open space, formerly a walled pleasure ground. Streamline, verandah railings and stairs in front of the round-topped, canopied and screened windows and an exterior marble pay box are later additions.

The ornate interior is carried out in a grand Edwardian manner. A triple-arched screen with ornate plaster decoration separates the entrance vestibule from a marble-floored lobby and ambulatory at the rear of the stalls; the latter decorated in a gilt and marble Rococo scheme, with exquisite, canopied kiosks at either end. (illustrated on page 58) Formerly, it was furnished with statuary and elaborately carved settees. Access to the stalls is through three domed arches; the central one with portraits of great literary figures including Shakespeare, Burns and Tennyson but no musicians, the outer two with patterned foliage decoration. In the three-level auditorium, the ceiling, proscenium, circle and balcony fronts are all finished in richly moulded plasterwork, some parts still retain their gilding. (illustrated on page 23) Originally, a crystal crown was suspended in front of the proscenium, a Star of India fixed each side of the stage and chandeliers hung overhead. Only the chandeliers remain in situ. Boxes with richly polished woodwork and gilding survive at the rear of the stalls, but three tiers of boxes along both sides have been removed and boarded over. These had handsome carved stone dados at ground level and decorated wooden fronts above.

When first opened, the seating was wood-backed; the replacement red plush seats are still present, but broken and dusty. Despite being empty for over ten years, the interior is largely intact and has retained all its backstage facilities including a scenery dock accessible through huge doors in the side wall.

A Souvenir Book[12] issued in 1924, explains how the building was in use long before its completion:

> At the time there were only the four external walls of the building then erected. These bare walls, for the purpose of holding a show, were disguised with drapery, whilst carpets cunningly laid down, served effectively to hide the fact that the floor was of mere earth!

→ The Royal Opera House (illustrated in the 1924 Souvenir Book) showing the now demolished corner tower and original single figure surmounting the pediment. The figure of Britannia, which has so far not been removed, can be seen on the rear corner to the right of the tower.

Reporting its early use as a cinema, the book continues:

> ...within an extraordinary short time (of the laying of the foundation stone in 1910) the place was opened for 'Kinemacolor' exhibitions in connection with the Coronation of King George V and the unveiling of the Queen Victoria statue.

At first the Royal Opera House shows were primarily live drama and high-class variety, the building being leased to visiting artists and companies for both evening and separate matinee shows. Top drama companies and individual artistes from Europe provided an exclusive programme for wealthy Bombay socialites. Bandman's own Opera Company performed here in the 1920s. The Souvenir Book describes the theatre in its hey-day:

> On a play night, all roads lead to the Royal Opera House, where, on alighting, a veritable palace of light greets the eye of the visitor. Then, as the foyer is reached a most charming effect, produced by the soft and scintillating lights from two magnificent crystal glass chandeliers, and two strikingly handsome illuminants, designed after the 'Star of India' is in evidence. The ceilings in the foyer, the ticket offices, cloakrooms, and so on, all have their setting in a charming scheme of decoration which is worked out in mauve and silver. From this dazzling domain of light the auditorium is entered...the Palace of Light has now given way to the Palace of Delight wherein every achievement in material, design and technique so much in evidence in the former, in the latter is manifested on an even more extensive and elaborate scale.

↑ *The vestibule leading to the stalls (from the 1924 Souvenir Book)*

↑↑ *The painted and gilded dome above the central entrance to the stalls.*

The theatre auditorium was cooled by a combination of fans and a system whereby air passed over blocks of ice before being pumped out through iron-grated floor channels. On a hot evening, the garden at the side of the theatre provided a refreshing retreat for those attending a performance. Of this, the Souvenir Book waxes lyrical:

> Here giant coconut palms sway pliantly in the sea breeze borne in from the adjacent Back Bay, whilst a profusion of other tropical trees and greenery, amidst which are dotted fountains and statuary, all add to the charm and attractiveness of this delightful spot - at all times a haven of peace, concord and goodwill.

The later Back Bay reclamation scheme would deprive the theatre of its proximity to the sea.

How frequently films were presented in these years is not known, although the Souvenir Book mentions that the boxes at the rear of the stalls "... are usually in great demand on the occasion of special cinematograph performances on account of their advantageous position." Pathé took over the management of the theatre in 1924 and its advertising promised that the Royal Opera House, under its new name, Pathé Cinema, would ".... in future be the real rendezvous of all lovers of pictures". Films were shown in the evenings, whilst matinee performances offered popular Hindi, Marathi and Gujarati dramas. In May 1927, the first demonstration in India of a process invented by Dr Lee DeForest for synchronising sound with picture called 'Phonofilm' took place here. The programme included a film of the actor Basil Gill playing a scene from *Julius Caesar*. From 1929 until their demise in 1932, Madan Theatres Ltd. leased the building for mixed programming of film shows and live drama; the venue reverting to its original name.

After 1935, the Royal Opera House enjoyed a spell as a first-run house for Warner Bros.-First National Pictures. Their advertisements offered "A New-Style Show in a New-Style Theatre!" with the innovation of running three shows a day and all seats, including the very cheapest, bookable in advance. Although now a full-time cinema, live productions continue to appear from time to time. By the end of the Second World War, however, slumping receipts forced the owner, J. F. Karaka, to seek a mortgage on the property from the Bank of Baroda, eventually selling out to the Maharajah of Gondal in 1952. For the next thirty years, during which time the theatre was managed by the Ideal Pictures Company, the cinema flourished, but after the mid-1980s attendances fell dramatically and the cinema ceased to be viable.

Since closure on 2nd February 1991, the structure has received basic maintenance. An application has been made for permission to demolish and build a shopping complex on the site, but the Royal Opera House is legally protected from alteration or demolition and a scheme has recently been put forward to finance the restoration of the theatre by building an office or apartment block on the adjacent land; however, this has not yet received approval.

↑ (left) *A notice in* The Times of India *of 1911 reporting the interruption of one of the first film shows at the Royal Opera House – a 'Kinemacolor' presentation by Bandman(n)'s Eastern Circuit.*

↑ (right) *An advertisement in* The Times of India *in 1924 with the venue's newly adopted name, Pathé Cinema, following the firm's takeover of the management of the theatre.*

Imperial

Sardar Vithalbhai Patel Road

Is there a more dramatic entrance to any cinema in India? Two life-sized, stone elephants, surmounted by a classical entablature in the form of a linked, double howdah, guard the archway leading to a partially covered courtyard. On the entrance arch is the word "Welcome" and in the keystone a monogram with the superimposed letters "N. M. T.".

The history of this building is puzzling: the fabric of three different styles is incorporated into the structure. Parts of a 19th-century Gothic edifice are present, including moulded arches and a short but elaborately decorated, crocketed spire. To one side of the entrance, a section of wall displays the words "(God Save) the King" (which must refer to Edward VII) with a unicorn on one side and suggestions of a lion on the other. This, together with a number of other classical features may date from the time when the building was used a theatre; its name is not known but the entrance monogram is a possible clue. Subsequent Hindu decoration probably date from a time when it may have served as a Temple or possibly a residence.

This is the second theatre in Bombay called the Imperial. By the early 1910s, the first Imperial Theatre, then located in Charni Road, was presenting a mixture of film shows and stage dramas. An early programme advertised the film *The God of the Sun* accompanied by several short Pathé items from France and a play. In 1916, the refusal of the Bombay Improvement Trust, owners of the land on which the cinema stood, to grant a new lease forced it to close and seek new premises elsewhere. Eventually the present location was chosen: the compound known as the Sri Mangaldas House facing what was then called Lamington Road. The existing building, partly converted and partly rebuilt, opened as the (new) Imperial Cinema in 1917; its external walls embellished with cartouches enclosing the letters "I.C.". However, for a time after Independence the name was changed to Swastik - still displayed on a few old notice boards – but later it reverted to the original.

The elephant gateway having fallen into disuse, the auditorium is now approached through an arch surmounted by a broken pediment, with the ticket office *(illustrated on page 58)* in a leafy garden courtyard; this is, in effect, an exterior foyer with seats for waiting under the trees.

The cinema accommodates 816 in stalls and balcony; the latter reached by an external staircase and roofed verandah supported by elaborately carved pillars. The auditorium walls and ceiling are partly covered with acoustic tiles, but around the proscenium and over the doors are examples of decorative plasterwork with stripped classical mouldings.

→ *The original entrance flanked by life-sized elephants supporting an arch in the form of a howdah.*

Regal

Opposite Museum, Colaba

The origin of the Regal is described graphically in the Golden Jubilee brochure[13] issued by the owners in 1983:

> In 1932 Globe Theatres acquired the old Saluting Battery site near the Gateway of India, from where gun volleys thundered greetings to Royalty, Viceroys and Governors who arrived in this *Urbs Prima in Indis*. And it was here that Bombay's first luxury theatre the Regal was erected in 1933.

The Regal was developed by Globe Theatres Ltd., the circuit run by Framji Sidhwa and K. A. Kooka, to provide a prestigious venue for both live drama & film presentation. It remains in the same family ownership. The architect and engineer was Charles F. Stevens, son of Frederick W. Stevens, the architect of Bombay's Victoria Terminus. Little is known about Charles Stevens - his R.I.B.A. nomination papers in 1907 state he was 34 years old and working as an assistant in his father's office in India. He is credited with designing the Orient Club in Bombay in 1912.

The opening ceremony, performed by the Governor of Bombay Sir Frederick Sykes, took place on 14th October 1933 and was followed by a Laurel & Hardy film *The Devil's Brother*. Occupying a prominent position opposite the Wellington Fountain, the cinema is a reinforced concrete structure, the front elevation in an Art Deco Aztec style with the name of the cinema in vertically placed letters flanked by narrow vertical windows surmounted by heroic sculpted heads. The exterior has been little changed since opening apart from a pale yellow colour wash and a replacement canopy. An integral underground car park was part of the original plan. According to the opening brochure[14] "....an entrance from the car park into the foyer of the theatre enables car-owners to reach their cars without going outside, a welcome feature in the monsoon".

↑ *The cover of the Souvenir Brochure for the Inauguration in 1933.*

← *A 1930s illustration of the cinema reflects its sophisticated, upmarket image.*

→ *The auditorium with its original decoration by Karl Schara. (photo-graphed for the inaugural brochure)*

Extensive alterations in the entrance lobby and foyers have resulted in these areas losing most of their original decoration. Extant is the marble staircase with teak panelling leading to the balcony foyer and a (possibly later) etched mirror depicting the figure of Oscar. However, changes in the auditorium are far more destructive. The original decorative scheme designed by a Czech artist, Karl Schara, was in "... an advanced modernistic style". To quote the opening brochure:

> The vast ceiling of the auditorium is carried out in pale cream, which deepens into orange as it curves down to the frieze which conceals the ceiling lights.... On the walls the lamps are of cubist design, in frosted glass. The ray pattern of these lamps is continued in the ceiling high wall panels, giving an astonishing illusion of great height..... From floor to ceiling the stage is surrounded by a striking cubist border in relief.

The removal of this decor took place during renovations in 1953, when the seating was changed to the current 1,178. Except for a teak dado, the auditorium was clad entirely in acoustic tiles, although still visible at the rear of the stalls are mouldings of a scroll of film and two theatrical masks - male and female, both representing comedy.

The Regal has been described as Framji Sidhwa's chef d'oeuvre and its many claims to fame include being the first in India to provide an underground car-park, first to introduce neon signs, first to employ uniformed staff and first to install Cinemascope. The Regal's projection box is one of the few in India to have installed a platter system.

A prized document in the Company's archive is a letter from Cecil B. DeMille complimenting the exhibitors on the record thirty-one weeks 'House Full' run of his 1956 epic *The Ten Commandments*. The cinema was in the news twenty-five years later, when it won a judgement in the Supreme Court overturning State restrictions on the distribution of Richard Attenborough's film *Gandhi* (1982).

In addition to screening first-run American and British films, many famous performers appeared live at the Regal. In the 1930s, Rabindranath Tagore presented recitals of his poems, the Bombay Symphony Orchestra gave regular concerts under the baton of its founder Mehli Mehta, a amateur violinist and father of the conductor Zubin Mehta. More recently, Ravi Shankar performed here and visiting overseas artistes includes the violinist Yehudi Menuhin, the opera singer Marian Anderson and the piano virtuosi Claudio Arrau and Rudolf Serkin. Another visitor to the Regal was President Nasser of the United Arab Republic, who presided at the Filmfare Awards in 1961. Prime Minister Jawaharlal Nehru was a regular patron when in Bombay. Framji Sidhwa also recalled visits to the theatre by various Maharajas and Nawabs:

> The Maharajas had a strange tendency. They would book two or three rows of Balcony seats and all the boxes completely, though only eight or ten people would turn up to occupy them. This was to prevent any of the 'commoners' from sitting anywhere near them and casting their eyes on the Maharanis. These Maharanis used to be in purdah.[15]

The cinema staff looked forward to these visits as they were assured of large tips from the Royal purse.

→ *The exterior of the Regal. The entrance to the integral car park is to the right of the main entrance.*

Eros

Maharshi Karva Road

↑ *Two advertisements of 1938 promoting the new cinema, restaurant and ballroom.*

← *A detail of the reliefs on one of the columns in the foyer.*

↓ *The exterior before an extra floor was added to the flanking office wings. (photographed c. 1950)*

The Eros was built by Shiavax Cambata, a Parsee entrepreneur from Karachi, and the cinema is still owned by a family trust. Cambata's sumptuous Art Deco flat, situated at the top of the tower, offered magnificent views over the city, whilst in the luxuriously appointed preview theatre on the floor below, the owner hosted private screenings for Bombay high society.

Built with American assistance, the building is a large multi-use structure of shops and offices and once included a restaurant and ballroom that could accommodate 500 dancers. The foundation stone was laid in 1935 and the cinema opened in 1938. Monumentally imposing outside, cool and elegant within, this expensively fitted venue was designed by the Bombay architect Sorabji Keikhushru Bhedwar and the artist responsible for the interior decoration was Fritz von Drieberg. The assertive Art Deco exterior is partially faced by red sandstone from Agra with the same tint used for the colour wash on the mouldings and ornamental details, whilst the remainder of the structure is rendered and painted light cream.

The Eros is at the end of an unbroken line of extravagant Art Deco apartment blocks facing one side of the Maidan. Built on a triangular site, two flanking wings are rounded off by the central corner entrance of the cinema. Between perforated *chajjas* – installed later when an extra floor was added to the office accommodation - a dramtic, semi-hexagonal block rises to finish as a stepped, circular tower. The name of the cinema appears in large Art Deco lettering above the entrance. From here, a small lobby leads into the magnificent circular foyer. Finished in black and white marble, the inlaid floor is a series of concentric circles complemented by a circular three-storey light well enclosed by sunburst

flares and chrome-plated railings. Marble columns decorated with blue and silver Art Deco reliefs depict figures from classical mythology. Access to the balcony is by marble stairs or lifts with black doors decorated with chrome strips suggestive of stylised waterfalls.

The air-conditioned, 1024-seat auditorium is on two levels. Blue and silver panels imitating a classical frieze run the full length of both side walls. These portray various activities involved in film making: actors in contemporary and historical costume, a producer with a glamorous female star lolling on his desk, shooting a scene, sound recording, prop-making and film editing are a just a few of the scenes depicted. Doors either side of the screen are framed by black polished granite surrounds with a clock and elongated Art Deco grilles above. The small curved stage has been retained but without a curtain and black embrasures surround the 70mm screen within a simple rectangular proscenium. No longer extant are murals depicting tropical vegetation and views of the Taj Mahal and Indian temples. The walls are now painted over in flat blues and greys and a fibrous acoustic cladding covers the ceiling.

↑ (left) *The auditorium during restoration work in 2001. Above timber scaffolding which covers the entire ceiling area, work is in progress outside performance hours.*
.

↑ (right) *A section of the wall relief depicting a gesticulating director and a camera crew shooting a scene.*

← *The stalls foyer.*

→ *The central tower - the culmination of the Eros façade.*

Metro

Mahatma Ghandi Road

Inaugurated with a Gala Performance of *Broadway Melody of 1938*, starring Eleanor Powell and George Murphy, the Metro opened in March of that year. *(illustrated on page 28)* It was planned by MGM primarily as a showcase for the studio's own films in the heart of what was then the commercial capital of British India. The Metro is an American-style movie house run until the late 1970s by MGM itself, after which they sold out to a local business. The building was designed by the Scottish-born, New York-based architect Thomas White Lamb (1871-1942), in association with another Scottish architect, David William Ditchburn (1883-1953), a principal in the Bombay practice of Ditchburn & Mistry. Lamb designed two cinemas in India, both for MGM: this one in Bombay and before that, another Metro in Calcutta.

Born in Dundee, Lamb emigrated as a child with his parents to Canada before settling in New York. At the precocious age of 21, he had an architectural office in New York and a listing in the 1892 Directory of the American Institute of Architects, some years before graduating in 1898 with a Bachelor of Science degree. Although his studies included mechanical drawing and acoustics, it is not apparent that he obtained any formal architectural qualifications. Prominent among his enormous output of over three-hundred buildings are many, major motion picture theatres in North America. He was also responsible for cinemas in other countries: Mexico, South Africa, Egypt, Australia and in Britain, the Empire Theatre, Leicester Square in London.

Lamb usually favoured historical styles especially Adam Revival, but his later output incorporated looser Rococo decoration. Paradoxically one of his theatres - Loew's 175th Street Theatre in New York - included elements of Hindu and Oriental inspiration. This is not present in his Indian cinemas, where, as in many commissions outside North America, Lamb employed a refined Art Deco styling.

The Metro remains much as Lamb envisioned, externally generally unaltered, but inside some decorations have been modified or lost. Built on a rectangular site, the six-storey block of reinforced concrete construction includes shops at ground level with offices in sections of the building isolated from the cinema auditorium. An imposing Art Deco tower with strong vertical ribs, a stepped top and American style vertical sign crowns the corner entrance front. Dwivedi and Mehrotra describe the luxurious Metro, as originally built:

> The Metro's interiors were aesthetic and stylish. The grand auditorium was approached from the marble foyer beyond the main staircase by four aisle entrances. The cinema equipment and the chairs and carpeting were all imported from America. The colour theme in the auditorium was red with pinkish shades for floors, ceiling and furniture. The most striking ornamental features were large mural paintings on either side of the auditorium, executed by students of the Bombay J. J. School of Art under the supervision of the Director, Charles Gerrard.[16]

From the entrance lobby, with pay boxes and attraction displays in streamlined, polished aluminium surrounds, patrons enter a large marbled-floored, double-height foyer.

→ *Two views of the auditorium – the moulded plasterwork is now painted in bright contrasting colours..*

Reeded, polished teak pilasters reach to a coffered ceiling, classical in design and decorated with a frieze and Greek motifs in roundels, all suggestive of Lamb's characteristic Adam style. Originally, light flooded in through the wall of glass along one side, but this is now painted over and curtained for security. Also missing are the streamline sofas, made by the Bombay firm of Wimbridge & Company. Three large cylindrical aluminium and glass chandeliers, of pronounced Art Deco styling with somewhat more than a hint of classicism, provide soft illumination. A marble staircase leads to the balcony foyer and a disused soda fountain and bar; aluminium railings in geometric patterns enclose the foyer well.

The auditorium has 1,491 seats on two levels. The ceiling decoration of vigorous, moulded patterns of zigzags and quadrants are now painted in rather garish contrasting reds and blues. Fretted grilles in the proscenium embrasures suggest the presence of an organ, but apparently one was not installed and the later wide screen obscures some of this decoration. When the cinema opened, the auditorium and foyer walls possessed murals depicting Vedic jungle scenes echoing Hindu epic mythology; these have all been removed.

The Metro's projection box is equipped with two Westrex Hi-Lite-130s and a Dolby sound system.

← *An artist's impression of the Metro's double-height foyer as it appeared in 1938. (from a contemporary brochure)*

→ *The exterior of the Metro with its American-style, vertical sign on the corner tower.*

Liberty
Opposite Bombay Hospital
Marine Lines

Construction of the Liberty cinema started in 1947, but the building had only reached the first-floor level when in 1948 its British architect, M. A. Riddley Abbott, died in a plane crash. The project was completed under the supervision of the Calcutta-based architect John Berchmans Fernandes (1905-1992) and the designer and architect W. M. Namjoshi was responsible for the main exterior elevations and the interior design. The Liberty is generally regarded as the latter's masterpiece.

Born at Ratnagari in Maharashtra, Waman Moreshwar Namjoshi (1907-1985?) does not seem to have had any formal architectural training, but after working as an assistant factory foreman and draughtsman, he joined his younger brother Vishnu in 1927 to produce designs for furniture and interior decoration. The business, trading as Nambros, was something of an over-night success and was soon obtaining commissions for palaces, offices and private residences; Namjoshi's elaborate and ostentatious decoration proved exceptionally popular with these wealthy clients. Commissions from cinema owners soon followed and over a period of forty years he produced designs for about thirty cinemas, including five where he was *de facto* his own architect as well. He also ventured into film design; in 1944, he created the lavish settings for the Shantaram production *Parvat Pe-Apna Dera*.

The Liberty, named in honour of Indian Independence, opened on 2nd February 1950 and, apart from a period of twenty years when it was rented out to another exhibitor, has been owned and managed by the Hoosein family.

← W. M. Namjoshi's design for the exterior of the Liberty.

↑ *The souvenir brochure for the 1950 Gala Inauguration.*
← *The stalls foyer and staircase to the balcony.*

↑ *Detail of the stylised fountain at the side of the proscenium.*

On a large rectangular site, the cinema is part of a six-storey building incorporating shops and offices. *(illustrated on page 10)* The office entrance has the name 'Liberty Building' in attenuated Art Deco letters above the doorway. On the cream and white front elevation, concrete pilasters rise from first-floor level through four storeys and at one corner an arching concrete bracket supports a fin-like vertical sign incorporating the cinema name and a pattern resembling piano keys. External booking office windows have decorative grilles and marble surrounds. Nowadays, the area in front of the building is enclosed by metal railings and patrolled by uniformed security guards.

From the entrance doors, through the foyers, the bar and stairs, the cinemagoer is transported into a world of elegance, comfort and sophistication. The doors are of inlaid teak and in a stepped pattern, a design repeated throughout the cinema. The foyers, illuminated by recessed lighting, are decorated with reeded teak panelling, moulded and painted plasterwork and a replacement deep red carpet has been woven in the original colour. A mirror-walled soda bar with built-in sofas provides luxurious waiting accommodation. The stairs to the balcony divide at a half-landing, where a tall Art Deco style mirror is surmounted by a black square-faced clock. The solid banisters and dado consist of alternate verticals of reeded teak and illuminated frosted glass.

All this however is overshadowed by the 1,196-seat auditorium: on the walls, ceiling and balcony are illuminated stepped bands of soft yellow and orange cove lighting with three large recessed circles in the centre of the ceiling.

→ *The auditorium with the main house lights turned down showing the indirect lighting display.*

An elaborate arch shape floats above the simple rectangular proscenium and over the spectacular, back-lit, stylised fountains either side. The drop curtain is of pink silk. Everywhere the decoration is delicate and refined, finished in a subtle scheme of soft browns, buffs and creams. Seating is arranged in stalls and balcony with a private box of five seats behind a glass screen at the rear.

Approached from the office entrance, at the top of the building is a private cinema. *(illustrated on page 57)* On a single steep rake are forty-two luxuriously upholstered, leather armchairs, each with a built-in writing table. The original owner was a music lover and, as was hinted in the vertical sign outside, a musical theme pervades the decorative scheme. Walls are clad with pilasters embellished with gilded piano keys and metal scrollwork topped by sconce uplighters. The barrel-shaped ceiling is decorated with a series of overlapping, scalloped coves painted with stylised foliage; indirect lighting is used to produce different coloured effects. The curtain is embroidered with a design incorporating a keyboard, stars & musical notation. Two original 1950 Bauers are still used in the projection box. Here is a gem fit for the reception of Louis B. Mayer himself!

↑ *The Liberty preview theatre – the embroidered curtain continues the musical theme of the décor.*

Apsara

(demolished)

The cinema is the favourite medium of entertainment today. It is the one vehicle which is capable of transporting us to a ringside seat to view and to experience some rare moments of enjoyment...to laugh spontaneously at the silly oddities of life, to live the emotions of a pair of young sweethearts or to view the epic battles that were fought in bygone eras of chivalry. It was with this in mind that I designed the Apsara cinema. My aim was to see that the design reflected these characteristics in a bold and truthful manner and in a contemporary style...My choice fell on an abstract composition of mobile and fluid forms.[17]

In this note in the inaugural brochure, the architect of the Apsara, Yahya Cassumjee Merchant (1903-1990), described the origins of his design as an interpretation of the fantastical elements of cinema itself rather than in terms of following any particular architectural style. However, contemporary reviews pointed out the similarities of Merchant's design with that of Oscar Niemeyer's work in Brazil, in particular, the Church of St Francis of Assisi at Pampulla (1943).

The 1200-seater cinema opened in 1965. *(auditorium illustrated on page 45)* Its rendered façade was decorated with pargetting of laurel leaves and a statue of the cinema's namesake, Apsara, portrayed as a celestial nymph. A soaring 30-metre high pylon displayed the name of the venue in large modernist letters. Inside, the central area of the double-height foyer was given over to a bubbling, blue-tiled pool from which emerged black columns rising to the ceiling. A spiral ramp provided access to the balcony foyer and drum-shaped bronzed downlighters flooded the space with warm light.

After operating for a mere twenty years, the cinema closed and before the building re-opened as a supermarket, the interior was gutted and the pylon dismantled. The remainder of the façade survived the supermarket's subsequent closure, but the end came in 2000 when the structure was flattened for redevelopment.

↑ *The exterior of the Apsara (from a photocopy of the inaugural brochure)*

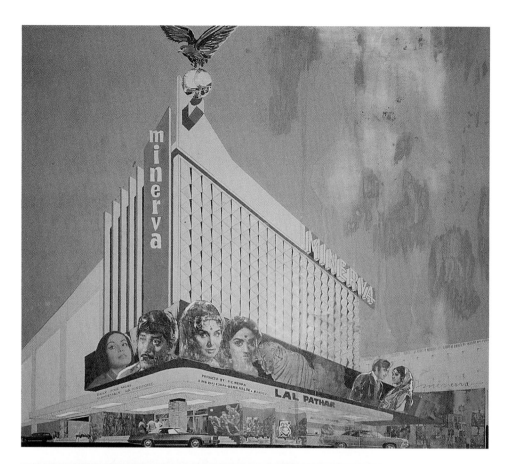

Minerva

Dr Dadasaheb Shadkamkar Marg

This large cinema seating 1,501 opened in 1972 replacing a previous Minerva Cinema, a converted theatre of c.1912 built in a classical style on the same site. The new cinema was designed by the Prabhu Parik Architectural Practice of Bombay with interiors by W. M. Namjoshi. In 2000, the Parik firm is planning its conversion into a multi-screen venue. The cinema is owned by a production company, Eagle Films, which has established a vertically-integrated business involved in all aspects of film production, distribution and exhibition. It also owns the Plaza in New Delhi.

The façade is studded with small concrete pyramids and topped by a wide brown fascia increasing in height at one corner, where originally a giant stone eagle stood atop a globe. This was later removed to avoid costly maintenance.

Flower-filled vases set on square white plinths line the long entrance lobby cum foyer; its low ceiling is part mirrored and part exposed concrete beams painted black.

The auditorium is arranged as stalls and a large but graceful, cantilevered balcony. The decoration is subtle; the walls and ceiling are covered by panels of acoustic membrane perforated in a variety of amoebic and sinuous shapes. The dominant colours are buffs and browns. Narrow, multi-coloured light boxes are set in a stepped design along both side walls. The front of the cantilevered balcony has long, forward-thrusting wings either side of the central recessed projection box. Installed are two pairs of Ashcroft Suprexs and Photophone projectors along with Dolby sound. The giant screen has no proscenium, its white embrasures fill the entire wall; although a drop curtain is present, it is not in use.

In 1975, Ramesh Sippy's 70mm 'Curry-Western' *Sholay*, starring Amjad Khan, opened at the Minerva. It ran with full houses for more than five years and was up to then the most successful Indian film. It brought Hollywood-style merchandising to India and an edited version of the soundtrack was issued on an LP record. Publicised as "Guns and Gore", *Sholay* is a sort of Indian 'Spaghetti Western' and started a trend of violent Indian films.

↑ *The exterior of the original Minerva (photographed in c.1935)*

↑↑ *An advertisement for the Sushil Majumdar's film* Lal Patthar, *the inaugural presentation at the new Minerva in 1972.*

← *The architect's 1970 perspective for the new Minerva, which shows a somewhat different treatment of the façade to that eventually built but with the gigantic stone eagle in place.*

← *The auditorium – the projection box is housed in the central recessed section of the cantilevered balcony.*

Shalimar
Dr Eruchsshak Hakim Lane

Applied vertical bands imitating strips of film with frames and sprocket holes decorate the front wall of the building. Situated in a small courtyard behind a row of ramshackle lock-up shops which obscure the remainder of the cinema from the street, this iconic façade is all that advertises the location of the venue to passers-by. When the cinema opened in c.1975, it had an 1,050-seat auditorium on two levels. Later a floor was inserted over the stalls, the space underneath converted into shops and the auditorium now occupies the former circle with a seating capacity of 574.

The cinema is fronted by a shabby, over-bearing canopy and fascia, whilst underneath are boarded-up shops. An external staircase leads to the first-floor entrance. which opens directly into the mostly unaltered, former balcony foyer. A circular bar and seating area is set around a central column, at the top of which are painted dancers and Hindu motifs surrounded by concentric, recessed circles and sun rays. Behind a semicircle of built-in seats are etched and painted mirrors depicting caparisoned elephants.

These remnants of former glory contrast with the dismal auditorium, now a single floor. The walls and ceiling are covered with white, fretted acoustic tiles without a proscenium or curtain and the bare screen embrasures are painted white. The cinema, a venue for adult films, is in a rundown state with seats slashed and damaged, others with parts missing and in places the floor surface broken and crumbling.

→ *The Shalimar façade is decorated with vertical metal bands imitating strips of film.*

14. Kolkata/Calcutta

Calcutta was founded in 1690 by Job Charnock, an English merchant-trader employed by the East India Company. Captured by the Nawab of Bengal in 1756, the city was retaken by Clive the following year and in 1772 made the capital of British India. The administrative centre possesses an impressive array of 18th and 19th century classical buildings.

In 1911, Calcutta ceased to be the capital and thereafter gained a reputation as a hothouse of left-wing political activism and as a major cultural and artistic centre. Its film industry, located at Tollygunge, known colloquially as 'Tollywood', was one of the first in the country; however, with production limited mainly to films in Bengali, it lost almost half the potential audience at Partition when the northern part of Bengal became East Pakistan, later Bangladesh. The city's film industry never fully recovered commercially, but can lay claim to being the home of India's internationally most famous filmmaker, the director Sajayit Ray.

Today, Calcutta, renamed Kolkata in 2001, is a huge sprawling city of some thirteen million people, the capital of the State of West Bengal. About a third of its eighty cinemas are situated in two distinct localities: one, the old British entertainment district near the city centre and the other, in the area around the University.

Star Theatre

Bidhan Sarani

On 2nd October 1898, the first documented film show in Calcutta took place in this theatre, when according to an advertisement in the newspaper *Amrita Bazar Patrika*, a "Professor" Stevenson (sometimes referred to as Stevens) presented a number of short films to accompany a programme of live drama. One of the items was entitled *Living and Moving Pictures of London Life*. The shows were immensely popular and after a month, the programmes were supplemented by other titles. Advertised by the Star's "Player, Playwright and Actor-Manager", Amrital Basu, as "Actualities" and "Fakes", the films were screened between performances of his dramatic production *Babu*, and a variety act entitled *Miss Nelly Mountcastle Dancing Her Snake Number*. The films included *Railway Train in Full Motion, Death of Nelson* and *Mr Gladstone's Funeral*.

According to the *Calcutta Daily News*, the following year the theatre presented a season of "Opera with Sweet Songs (followed by) the Million's Favourite Feast, the Bioscope Exhibition of New Pictures". Spasmodic film presentations continued at the theatre until 1900 when all the Bioscope equipment was offered for sale as a job lot.

Hiralal Sen (1866-1917), a Bengali photographer, saw Stevenson's first show and with his assistance filmed short sequences from the Star Theatre's stage production *The Flower of Persia* and the resulting film was included in Stevenson's subsequent film shows. Later Sen acquired his own camera and projector from England and with his brother, Motilal, established a film production and exhibition business called the Royal Bioscope Company in 1899. Many of his early films included sequences of the theatre's dramas, which were shown as interval entertainment at Amar Dutta's Classic Theatre in Calcutta. In 1904, he made his only full-length feature, *Ali Baba and the Forty Thieves*, but the company was unable to survive the growing competition from Madan's Elphinstone companies and closed in c.1914: sometime previously, all Sen's films are thought to have been destroyed in a fire at his studio.

Dating from around 1865, the Star Theatre was one of the principal venues for Bengali drama in the city. It continued as a live house presenting Bengali social and mythological dramas until it closed in 1991 after a devastating fire. This left a burnt-out ruin with only the façade, front of house areas and lower part of auditorium's side walls standing.

The elaborately decorated, stone-faced exterior shows the influence of Hindu Temple architecture, but incorporates Mughal and Baroque features and Gothic windows as well. The lobby and grand staircase immediately behind the façade remain intact and are now inhabited by squatters. In the auditorium, all traces of seating have disappeared. The stalls area is smothered by dense vegetation sprouting out of the concrete floor and only the stepped ramp of the circle with its sweeping curved front is accessible. A few stone pillars with finely carved Corinthian capitals are left standing along each side and a stone roundel on the rear wall of the circle displays the theatre's initials. The stage and everything beyond has collapsed into a pile of rubble.

→ *The surviving façade of the Star Theatre.*

Globe
Nely Sengupta Sarani

The original theatre on this site, The Opera House, was financed by a group of prosperous English residents, who wanted to bring the best of European opera and drama to the city. It was built by the Scottish firm, Macintosh, Burn & Co. but although the name of the architect is not recorded, it may have been a Mr Osmond, who was the firm's chief designer architect at the time.

The theatre opened on 2nd November 1867 with a Gala Performance of Gounod's *Faust* given by Augusto Cagli's Grand Italian Opera Company, but the performance had to be abandoned in the third act after the roof was damaged in a storm. Undeterred, Cagli's Company staged a re-opening a few days later with a performance of Verdi's *Il Trovatore*. So rapturous was the reception, that the Company returned in each of the next five years to present further seasons of Italian opera. During a visit to Calcutta in 1876, the Prince of Wales, later King Edward VII, attended the theatre for an evening of "Indian and English Songs and Dances" along with a show called *Used Up* and is reported in the local papers to have played a movement from a Mozart symphony on the piano!

In 1899, the theatre was purchased by one of Calcutta's leading criminal lawyers and leased to Pemberton & Clifford Willard & Co. They turned it into a home for light opera and vaudeville shows, persuading Calcutta's leading impressario Maurice Bandman and his 'Revue Company of Beautiful Girls' - probably something like a Follies show - to move here from Calcutta's other prestigious venue, the Theatre Royal.

The Opera House was sold in 1906 to a Mr E. M. Cohen, who renamed it The Grand Opera House, promoting it as one of the top venues for touring vaudeville and musical acts from Britain. Seasons of Gilbert and Sullivan,

numerous appearances by celebrity performers from Europe and even prize fights were presented, but its heyday as a purely live theatre was coming to an end.

At Rangoon in 1915, two Parsees originating from Bombay, Framji H. Sidhwa (1880-1962) and Kaikhushroo A. Kooka formed The Globe Cinema Company (later Globe Theatres Private Ltd.) and on 3rd April opened their first cinema, called Globe Theatre, in a converted bicycle shop. According to Sidhwa's son Mancek, the name was chosen in honour of Shakespeare's Globe Theatre. Their business expanded rapidly and soon they were operating cinemas in many cities, firstly in Burma and later in India, whilst at the same time running film distribution agencies for some of the big Hollywood companies all over the Sub-Continent. Sidhwa was involved with film production as well, joining the Board of Bombay Talkies Ltd.

↑ *Kaikhushroo A. Kooka* (left) *and Framji H Sidhwa.*

→ *The Globe with the original Opera House façade (photographed in 1960) before it was swept away in the later 1960s rebuilding.*

→ *The original auditorium (photographed in 1930).*

In 1922, the Globe Cinema Company purchased Calcutta's Grand Opera House and after converting it to a cinema renamed it Globe Grand Opera House, later shortened to The Globe and subsequently just Globe. Few changes were made to the building and the richly decorated three-level auditorium was retained. A section of the 'gods' was removed and the space used for the projection box, this slightly reducing the overall number of seats from the previous total of around 850.

Lord Lytton, the Governor of Bengal, inaugurated the new cinema on 23rd November, its opening presentation being *A Sporting Double*, starring Douglas Munro and Lillian Douglas. The first talking picture shown in India, *Melody of Love*, was screened here in 1928. Although operating primarily as a cinema, mixed programming of films and live shows continued for many years. Visiting artistes included The London Revue Company, Rex Storey's Hollywood Revue, Ram Gopal, Uday Shankar's Ballet Company and a well-known magician called Professor Sorcar.

By 1964, the owners considered the cinema too old-fashioned for contemporary audiences and decided to undertake a complete modernisation. The venue was closed and the old theatre totally gutted, leaving only the structural shell of the auditorium standing. When the Globe reopened, it offered patrons luxurious, air-conditioned comfort, a giant Todd-AO screen and stereophonic sound. B. A. Mistry of Bombay was the architect and consulting engineer for this work. The first presentation was 20th Century-Fox's *Cleopatra*, starring Elizabeth Taylor and Richard Burton.

The original Opera House had a Baroque facade with a central pediment, balustrades and an ironwork verandah,

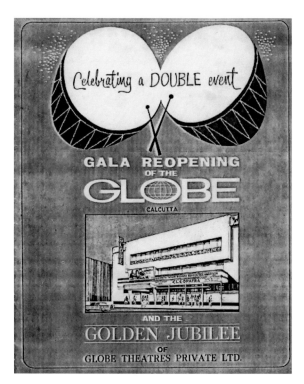

but these were all swept away in the 1960s rebuilding work. The new design comprised horizontal bands of windows above a prominent canopy supported on tapering piers, but this facade proved exceptionally short-lived: it was altered radically during further rebuilding in the late 1970s involving the removal of the canopy, the installation of new, huge vertical windows and shop fronts were

inserted either side of the cinema entrance. This façade has so far survived, but been subjected to many, unsympathetic alterations.

Inside, on the wall of the entrance lobby is a large etched glass mirror depicting a leaping figure in front of a globe. Although the foyer is expensively finished in marbles and decorative laminates, it has little other decoration but parts of the grand staircase from the earlier building have been incorporated in the new scheme. The 1,125-seat auditorium, now with a large cantilevered balcony, is a plain, box-like space clad in acoustic tiles, replacing the laminate used in the 1960s. The screen has no masking or proscenium, but a drop curtain is still used. A rather austere soda fountain and cafe dating from the time of the reconstruction is in poor decorative order. Changes to the auditorium are planned, which may involve twinning.

The cinema remains in the same ownership, which is run by the sons of the founders. The Company is one of the oldest surviving film exhibitors in India, although now reduced to three venues: the Globe and two in Mumbai: the Capitol and the Regal. Its motto is still "Nothing But The Best!"

↑ *Poster for the 20th Century-Fox film* Winged Victory *at the Globe in 1945*

← (top) *Poster for the 1937 London Revue Company season at the Globe.*

← *The Souvenir Brochure for the re-opening of the Globe in 1966 illustrates the new façade, which lasted less than fifteen years.*

→ *A perspective of the 1970s revamped façade (from an old photostat).*

Chaplin
Surendra Nath Banerjee Road

First opened as a drama theatre in the 19th century, this was the location for an early film presentation. In 1900, the then Actor-Manager, Ardhendusekhar Mustafi, exhibited a short Bioscope picture of scenes from one of his own stage productions, *Praphulla*. Following a change of ownership, in c.1907 it was purchased by the Elphinstone Picture Palace Company and converted into a full-time cinema - one of if not the first in Calcutta - taking the name The Elphinstone Picture Palace.

A production company, The Elphinstone Picture Palace Company (later, Elphinstone Theatrical Co and later still, Elphinstone Bioscope), ran the cinema as an outlet for its own films in the fashionable, British entertainment district of the city. The Elphinstone companies were owned by J. F. Madan & Sons, a firm run by a wealthy Parsee from Bombay, Jamsetti Framji Madan (1856-1923). He was involved in many aspects of the emerging film industry, also owning a theatre group and many other enterprises including a pharmaceutical company.

A larger than life showman, Madan was one of the first businessmen in India to appreciate the commercial potential of the new medium. Over some twenty years, he was to become India's first Hollywood-style movie mogul, running a huge company involved in all aspects of film production, distribution and exhibition. From about 1890, Madan was the actor-manager of a touring Parsee theatre company and after taking over two Bombay-based companies, the Khatau-Alfred and the Elphinstone, moved to Calcutta, where the companies were later merged and re-named the Elphinstone Theatrical Company.

His initial involvement with cinema began in 1902 when he started presenting films in tented cinemas on the Calcutta Maidan. By 1905, he was financing film productions using the actors in his own theatrical company and soon extended his activities by running a chain of temporary and later permanent cinemas in Calcutta. In 1919, he established Madan Theatres Ltd., which grew into India's largest film conglomerate and at its zenith in the late 1920s operated over one hundred and seventy cinemas on the Sub-Continent, including half a dozen in the centre of Calcutta. The Company's distribution agencies also controlled around half of all the films shown in the entire country.

After Madan died, the Company continued under the management of his five sons, but during the early 1930s its fortunes declined. A huge investment in sound

← Jamsetti Framji Madan (from an old photostat)

probably exists under several layers of later cladding. The present frontage takes advantage of the prominent corner site to display a large (originally articulated) neon figure of Charlie Chaplin with bowler hat and cane. The name Chaplin in big red lower-case lettering along one side of the building probably dates from the 1960s. A life-size plaster model of the comedian also stands in the foyer. Some of the interior décor dates from the 1930s: flush marble finishes, plaster mouldings and reeded woodwork, but its overall appearance is rather dour, possibly due in part to the 1960s makeover. The auditorium has 707 seats, all wooden in the stalls and cushion moquette tip-ups in the balcony, This has its original, curved marble front, but elsewhere little decoration has survived the various modernisations. The screen has no proscenium but still uses a drop curtain.

↑ *The Chaplin with the neon figure of Charlie Chaplin on the corner fin.*

equipment, problems with production finance and the failure to secure a tie-up with either Universal or Columbia Pictures all contributed to its demise. By 1933, they had sold all but one cinema and the Elphinstone was bought by the Modi family's Western India Cinemas Ltd.

Renamed Minerva after Sorab Modi's production company, the building was either drastically altered or even partially rebuilt with a new façade and front of house areas. After Independence the name changed again, this time to Chaplin, when along with other cinemas in the city it was nationalised by the State Government and leased back to a private exhibitor. Since 1990, it has been managed by The West Bengal Film Development Corporation, an autonomous body set up by the State Government.

Of the original theatre, almost nothing is visible today, though much of the structure of that building

Roxy Talkies
Chowringhee Place

Built in the 1920s as a drama theatre called the Empire, it was then owned by Humayan Properties Ltd. At one time this Calcutta-based business, which was later controlled by members of the Nepalese Royal Family, ran four other cinemas in India including the New Empire and Lighthouse in Calcutta.

Once the nearby Grand Opera House became a cinema, the Globe, touring repertory companies from Europe turned to the Empire, which for a few years took over the mantle as the most prestigious venue in the city for such performances. In 1925 the Gonzales Brothers' Italian Grand Opera Company performed a season of more than twenty operas here.

However, in 1936, the Empire was converted into a cinema under the name Roxy Talkies with live shows appearing only periodically until 1965. During the British period, the Roxy attracted the crème of Calcutta society to showings of English-language films and performances by major visiting artistes.

Situated on a corner site with two prominent street facades, the cement-rendered exterior is designed in a stripped style with a cupola above the curved corner entrance. The circular foyers are decorated in a sophisticated, streamlined Art Deco manner with reeded wooden dados, moulded recessed light fittings and doors of etched glass with decorative chrome fittings. A composition floor has quartered green and yellow concentric circles. In the circle foyer, the streamline décor is further embellished with stylised lotus flowers, now painted in sickly pinks. A circular lightwell opens to the balcony foyer above.

The three-level auditorium has 840 seats. The serpentine front of the circle is decorated with shallow mouldings; the balcony is a simple curve with slips along each side to the proscenium. Above dados of two contrasting, striped woods, the scalloped plasterwork on the walls and the moulded roundel in the centre of the ceiling have been repainted in a newly-devised colour scheme of vivid pinks, blues and yellows. The deeply moulded proscenium is treated similarly. A long-disused, red drop curtain has recently been restored and brought back into use. The cinema shows only first-run Hindi films from 'Bollywood'. It is now owned by the Mehta family of Mumbai, who also own the Paradise in Kolkata.

→ *The corner entrance of Roxy Talkies surmounted by a cupola.*

New Empire
Humayan Place

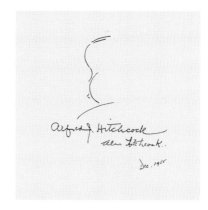

"New Empire - The Home of Warner Bros. Pictures" proclaims a dilapidated sign on a side wall of the building; a relic from the period after the Second World War when this cinema was run by a subsidiary of the Hollywood studio, principally as an outlet for their own product. *(illustrated on page 58)* Built by Humayan Properties Ltd. and initially managed by them as part of a small chain of theatres in the city, it reverted to the company after Warners left in the 1980s and remains in that ownership today.

The New Empire was fully equipped as a cinema from the start, despite possessing both the auditorium layout and extensive back-stage facilities of a live drama theatre. The name of the architect has not been established, but an unsigned perspective of the proposed façade dated 1927 presents an exuberant composition of decorative modernistic towers mixed with classical and Baroque details. Of brick construction with a concrete rendering, the exterior of the building is currently in poor condition and somewhat altered; the tops of the side towers have been mutilated, the middle one replaced by a mansard roof and the arcade glazing removed. The ground floor is let as general commercial space. Access to the cinema is through an entrance lobby, and up a monumental marble staircase to the first floor foyer and restaurant. However, what was once a richly ornate interior has been changed drastically and given a utilitarian makeover. All that survives in the front of house areas is a large Art Deco sculpture of a dancing female with a winged cherub and the staircase, both of which have been rebuilt in new positions. Only a tiny panelled lift was left untouched.

Acoustic improvements introduced in the auditorium ruined it aesthetically and almost every surface is now clad with tiling. The proscenium, side boxes and elaborately decorated, central dome are all present but boarded over and hidden from view, leaving the sweeping front of the circle the only feature unaffected. The orchestra pit still exists, but is sealed off. On opening, it seated 904 on three levels, since reduced to 828. During the 1990s, a 70mm screen was installed and the projection box now houses two adapted Westrex-14s in conjunction with a Dolby sound system.

In the Company Archive is a 'Golden Book' containing hundreds of autographs and goodwill messages; a nostalgic reminder of the many famous performers who appeared at the theatre until 1965 when live stage shows were discontinued. The signatories include Ravi Shankar, Yehudi Menuhin, Ruggiero Ricci, and members of famous European chamber groups. Other autographs are of film personalities such as Danny Kaye, Alfred Hitchcock and Raj Kapoor, all of whom made guest appearances to promote their films. Between film runs in the early years, performances of Shakespeare and other classics were given by touring repertory companies from Britain and throughout the 1930s, seasons were devoted to the plays of Rabindranath Tagore. During the Second World War and until Independence, British troops stationed in Calcutta were able to attend E.N.S.A. shows at the theatre; one such was advertised as *Laughs! Laughs!! And More Laughs!!!*. A percipient critic in the *Bombay Sunday Standard* reviewing the 1945 Ralph Reader Show commented, "The 'baby' of the show is Peter Sellers, aged 19, the boy-drummer and impressionist. A big future lies before him."[18]

↑ *The page in the 'Golden Book' signed by Alfred Hitchcock and his wife Alma during their visit to the cinema in 1955.*

→ *The unsigned perspective of the New Empire, dated 1927.*

Elite

Surendra Nath Banerjee Road

J. F. Madan's Elphinstone Bioscope Company opened a cinema here sometime before 1915. The name, The Palace of Varieties, suggests the building may have had an earlier incarnation as a live variety theatre, but no evidence has been found to confirm this. When the Madan firm ceased trading in the 1930s, the cinema was sold to Western India Cinemas Ltd. and in 1938 the name was changed to Elite.

Concurrent with his work remodelling the same firm's flagship venue, the New Empire in Bombay, the architect M. A. Riddley Abbott was supervising an even more extensive transformation here. After Riddley Abbott's death in 1948, the locally based architect John Berchmans Fernandes completed the project and was entirely responsible for the interior decoration.

"All new but the name!" trumpeted the Elite's re-opening advertising in 1950: the first presentation in the new theatre was Howard Hawks' *Red River*, starring John Wayne and Montgomery Clift. Whilst retaining parts of the outer walls and some floors, the cinema now presents an elegant Art Deco appearance both outside and in. The asymmetrical frontage is finished in a concrete render painted cream and red with the name in large lower-case letters above horizontal banding and in neon letters on the prominent vertical fin, but, nowadays, huge attraction posters obscure most of the facade above the canopy.

The foyer is in a restrained Moderne streamlined style. The floors are marble, the dados, wall panels and doors are of two contrasting woods set in reeded bands and the ceiling recesses, of intersecting moulded circles, house indirect lighting. A mirror in a stepped black marble surround extends the full height of the stairwell to the balcony foyer. The décor in the soda fountain is still more dramatic; behind a semi-circular bar of backlit glass blocks is a large etched mirror depicting a fountain and fishes. Built-in settees with exaggerated armrests are contemporary.

The auditorium has 1,228 seats, rexine covered tip-ups in the balcony and more recent, red plastic in the stalls. A streamline feature of stepped and moulded plaster, indirectly illuminated by white light - somewhat reminiscent of décor in a George Coles' Odeon - runs down the centre of the ceiling ending in a bull-nose shape above the screen. The walls, finished in soft shades of orange and yellow, echo the design of the foyer, further embellished with metal grilles of stylised vine leaves. When opened, the cinema had a simple rectangular proscenium with rounded corners. To accommodate the wide Cinemascope screen, this was removed and a new proscenium with shallow mouldings installed. The small wooden stage was retained and the drop curtain is still in use. Originally, the blue of the ceiling deepened towards the screen end, but this is no longer apparent. At this cinema, exceptionally, indirect lighting effects throughout the building are in working order. The projectors are upgraded c.1965 Fedixit T-70s, imported from Italy, with a Dolby sound system and a c.1965 Klangfilm mono amplifier as backup.

Within the building is a 50-seater preview theatre that is no longer used and on the top floor is the owner's office, a small but exceptionally elegant room with panelled walls of contrasting woods and complementary furniture of the period.

→ *The Art Deco exterior of the Elite - nowadays mostly hidden behind large attraction posters.*

↑ *Flyers advertising forthcoming attractions at the Elite in 1942* (left) *and 1941.*

↑ *The Elite auditorium in 1950 with the original small proscenium and the bull-nose ceiling decoration displaying its concealed lighting effect. (from an old photostat of the opening brochure)*

Mitra

Bidham Sarani

Birendranath Sarkar, known as B. N. Sircar (1901-1980), trained as a civil engineer at London University and upon his return to India established a successful architectural and construction business in Calcutta. His commissions included work on a number of theatres and whilst engaged on one of these, he is reputed to have decided to build his own cinema. This was to be the Chitra and the leading Nationalist politician Subhas Chandra Bose performed the opening ceremony on 30th December 1930.

Sircar's next move was into film production, setting up International Filmcraft and soon after, New Theatres in Tollygunge, later nicknamed Calcutta's 'Tollywood'. Filmcraft produced two silent films, *Chorekanta* and *Chashar Meye* (both 1931), which were shown at the Chitra cinema accompanied by the music of Rabindranath Tagore performed by a pit orchestra under the baton of Raichand Baral. Sircar had a somewhat chequered career. His early efforts were apparently flops, but later he produced several films adapted from the works of major Bengali writers which were better received. His company went on to make a string of financially successful but routine, family pictures, employing amongst many notable directors, Debaki Bose and Charu Ray. Sircar's lasting achievement was to introduce Western-style professionalism to the Indian film industry. In the early 1930s, Wilford Deming, an American technician employed by Sircar, but previously working with Irani in Bombay, reported:

> Calcutta provided a complete surprise, contrasting with the rushing, haphazard methods of Bombay. Here I was presented with the nucleus of what has become a real production unit, well financed andwith an ambitious programme of producing pictures for India comparable to those of the independent Hollywood companies.[19]

Once the Chitra was open for business, Sircar built another cinema for himself, the New Theatre, in a more fashionable, city-centre location. This venue, since renamed New Cinema, still exists but was extensively altered in 1973. During Sircar's time, the Chitra ran Bengali-language films including those from his own studio, whilst the New Theatre exhibited English-language and occasionally Hindi films. The production company folded in 1954.

↑↑ *The logo of New Theatres Ltd. incorporated an elephant head.*

↑ *B. N. Sircar in c.1930.*

The Mitra family purchased the Chitra cinema in 1963 and the current name was adopted. To the street, the cinema presents a symmetrical, banded and stepped façade and is one of the few in the city to possess a working neon sign. Entry is directly into the lobby cum foyer, a one and a half height cube with a gallery around three sides. Decorating the walls are large Henri Rousseau-like paintings of 1931 by Dabi Proshad Roy Chowdhury, which depict exotic and fanciful scenes of flowers, foliage and animals. These paintings were restored, or possibly repainted, by Shantonu Mitra in 1985. The logo of New Theatres, an elephant head, is present in the decoration throughout the cinema, most prominently in the form of large brass door handles.

The two-level auditorium has 1,158 seats and betrays its theatrical antecedents in the arrangement of the horseshoe-shaped balcony and slips. The balcony front has a narrow, embossed frieze and metal rails, but elsewhere, except for small areas of moulded plasterwork, most the original decoration is now obscured under later cladding. An embrasure with flanking abstract patterns has replaced the proscenium, but the curtain remains and is still in use. Staff wear military-style uniforms with the name of the cinema on the breast pocket.

← *The exterior of the Mitra at dusk with its neon sign illuminated.*

The Lighthouse
Humayan Place

The Lighthouse is a rare example in India of a cinema designed by a major European architect in the International Style, but it is unclear why this commission was awarded to the Dutch Master, Willem Marinus Dudok (1884-1974), architect to the town of Hilversum from 1916 responsible for housing, schools and most notably the seminal Town Hall (1928-30). His work-list records the project as "The Garden House and Lighthouse Cinemas," but the building only contains one major auditorium and this has always been known simply as The Lighthouse. A second auditorium - a small preview theatre - is no longer in use; maybe at the

↑ The laying of the foundation stone on 21st February 1938. Dudok, in the white suit, is standing to the right of the stone.

design stage this was the Garden House Theatre. The Lighthouse is Dudok's only major building on the Sub-Continent and was designed during 1934-38 for the Huyaman Properties Group, which already owned the adjacent New Empire. One other project, a house in Calcutta for a director of Humayan Properties is also mentioned, but it is uncertain whether this was ever built.

Dudok was in attendance when Mrs A. De Bois Shrosbree, the wife of the Chairman of the Company, laid the foundation stone on 21 February 1938. The contractors were the Scottish firm Mackintosh, Burn Ltd. and the Technical Advisors Von Geberen. It opened in 1939 with the John Cromwell film *Algiers* starring Hedy Lemarr and Charles Boyer and for many years exhibited only English-language films from Hollywood. It now shows both American films and blockbusters from 'Bollywood'.

The most dramatic architectural feature of the Lighthouse is the steel pylon in front of the building. Dudok, using the vocabulary of the Modern Movement, reinvented the traditional vertical theatre sign as a narrow free-standing girder rising to a great height directly from the pavement and finishing above the roofline of the cinema. Its only adornment is the name of the cinema in neon letters running down each side. The inspiration for this extraordinary feature is unknown, but local legend has it that Dudok was influenced by the steel girder structure of the massive Howrah Bridge which was then about to be built over Calcutta's River Hughli.

The Lighthouse has no other exterior decoration. Under a flat roof with a prominent overhang, the unadorned facades are of plain concrete rendering rather than Dudok's characteristic exposed brickwork, punctuated by long rows of metal-framed windows.

Only the treatment of the entrance, set back behind a square-pillared arcade, echoes the comparable arrangement of the New Empire next door; otherwise, there could scarcely be a greater contrast between two adjacent cinema buildings.

On a large corner plot, the 1,339-seater cinema is in a seven-storey building, which also accommodates two dance floors, one large enough to hold up to four hundred dancers, a restaurant and bar, preview theatre and offices. The ticket office windows have metal grilles with a lighthouse motif. Subsequent, unsympathetic changes have spoilt the interior, but Dudok's original intentions can be deduced from what remains. A lightwell enclosed by tubular steel rails once penetrated three foyer levels, but each of these is now completely floored over creating three separate spaces. A giant Art Deco clock face, intended to be seen from the lower foyer, is visible now only at close quarters. Stairwells and landings with tubular steel handrails and porthole windows connect the foyers to the disused and empty dance floors and bar.

The auditorium, comprising stalls and a large cantilevered balcony, escaped any major alterations until the introduction of Dolby sound in 1992, when it was clad in acoustic tiles. These concealed the wall design of shallow plaster arches, which are, apparently, intact underneath. Seat standards are decorated with stylised lighthouses. In the projection box are two Peerless Magnarc/Centurys and still present is the 1930s Mirrorphonic sound equipment.

Despite its less than glorious state, The Lighthouse remains one of the most important examples of the Modern Movement in India.

→ *Two views of the exterior of the Lighthouse.*

Metro
Jawaharlal Nehru Road

The Metro was the first cinema in India designed by Thomas White Lamb. It was built on the site of an earlier theatre of which only parts of the auditorium walls were retained. Here, Lamb employed a dramatic Art Deco scheme with none of his characteristic classical or Rococo decoration. In Lamb's Job-Book, the designs are dated 1934 and the cinema opened in 1935. The striking, stepped façade has a vertical neon sign at one corner and a canopy with the cinema's name in metal letters on its fascia. It is reminiscent of other MGM cinemas designed by Lamb for locations outside the United States or Canada and in particular like those in Adelaide in Australia and Santurce in Puerto Rico.

The foyer is palatial; an expensively furnished, double height space with a grand staircase sweeping up to the balcony foyer and gallery extending along two sides. Ribbed teak pilasters rise the full height of the walls to finish as elongated brackets supporting the stepped ceiling. The floors, dados and stairs are of marble. Polished metal banisters and railings of elaborate design enclose the stairs and galleries and large modernistic chandeliers of elongated hexagonal form illuminate this handsome interior. The ceiling of the balcony-level soda fountain and bar has indirect lighting in moulded concentric circles. Original, tubular steel furniture, small round-topped tables and padded chairs are all present.

In contrast, the auditorium conjures up a 1930s fantasy of an exotic, tented pavilion. The plaster finish has the appearance of fabric pleated and gathered in drapes and pelmets covering every available wall surface. It is painted in subtle gradations of buffs, pinks and mauves, which give an added realism to the three-dimensional effect. Pendant light fittings in the style of cylindrical lanterns hang from the ceiling, which has a less ornate, ribbed decoration. A deeply moulded proscenium encloses the stage and the red drop curtain is still used. On either side are three, tall, screened openings, which suggest the presence of pipe organ chambers; however, these are purely decorative as, apparently, a theatre organ was never installed. The auditorium has 1,208 seats, all cushioned and with decorative metal standards. In the projection box are Ashcroft Superpower projectors adapted for Cinemascope and the old Westrex A2 sound equipment has been superseded by a recently installed Dolby system.

When the Metro opened, the MGM management only showed English-language films, principally their own product and films handled by their Indian distributor. In 1972, the Hollywood Studio sold out to a local exhibitor and, subsequently, it has screened major, first-run Hindi films. In the last few years, the cinema has undergone extensive, internal restoration. Apart from a few acoustic tiles on the rear wall of the circle, the interior has been returned to something like its original 1930s splendour, confirming its status as one of the finest examples of Art Deco in India. The exterior awaits a comparable treatment.

← *The Metro exterior and vertical sign awaiting restoration in 2000.*

→ Page 138 overleaf (top): *The Metro's double-height foyer with a grand staircase sweeping up to the balcony and soda fountain.*

→ Page 138 overleaf (bottom): *The Metro's auditorium showing the decorative pipe chambers either side of the proscenium.*

Radha

Bidhan Sarani

Construction work started in 1944, but took ten years to complete and the cinema did not open until 1954. The building incorporates a block of flats with a central, recessed glazed stairwell rising four storeys. The entrance doors are original with geometric-patterned, etched glass and chunky, chrome-plated fittings.

The Moderne exterior appears restrained in comparison with the exuberant décor inside. In the foyers, large, moulded plaster forms with concealed lighting are painted in rich greens, purples and pinks. Decoration in the auditorium is even more pronounced; a profusion of ribbed and banded plasterwork painted in pinks, blues and browns. The deeply recessed proscenium and its curved embrasures are treated in a similar manner. A curtain is extant, but no longer used. The original ceiling design is obscured by later lattice boarding.

Most of the equipment in the projection box has been there since the cinema was built. The three Peerless Magnarc/RCA Excel projectors were manufactured in Glasgow in 1952 and a GEC mono value amplifier is still in working order, but nowadays only used for emergencies. The recently installed Westrex Ahuya Stereo equipment is now the main sound system.

The cinema seats 920 on two levels. For forty years, it screened only mainstream Bengali-language films, but since 1994, the programming policy has changed and it now targets the local resident and university audience, showing specially selected Hindi and occasionally English-language films.

→ *The central section of the Radha façade incorporating the four-storey stairwell.*

Prachi

A. J. C. Bose Rd

The Prachi dates from the early 1950s. At the junction of its two angled facades, a tall fin-like structure with horizontal quadrants at one time displayed the name of the cinema in neon. Now defunct, this has been replaced by a small sign in Bengali script.

Art Deco entrance doors with chrome-plated handles of geometric design have etched glass incorporating stylised bamboo. A large Indo-Deco style rondel in red, cream and blue enamels faces patrons as they enter the lobby. The floors in the foyers are of marble, the walls clad in reeded teak panelling and the ceilings decorated with large swirling plaster mouldings picked out in pastel colours. Luxurious areas for waiting still have the original, bulky, upholstered sofas.

In the auditorium, every surface exhibits playful decoration on plaster and plywood. Simple vertical sound baffles of shaped and painted plywood are fitted along the walls over patterns of diamonds and stars, chequerboard or zigzag panels, all painted in mauves, yellows and pinks. Embossed rectangles in pink, blue and cream cover the ceiling, pierced by irregular, moulded, amoebic-shaped recesses containing concealed lighting. The screen has a rectangular proscenium with simple mouldings and a tasselled, drop curtain.

The Prachi accommodates 800 in stalls and a circle; the seat rows identified only in Bengali script on flush, wooden standards. It is a first-run house for Bengali films.

↑ *The window and fin details of the Prachi are picked out in red; the remainder of the façade is off-white.*

→ *The Indo-Deco rondel in the lobby.*

Darpana
Bidhan Sarani

The cinema has a vertical sign with its name in Bengali script arranged on three large rosettes, but otherwise the exterior is unadorned with an asymmetrical, rendered façade pierced by long rows of steel-framed windows. A glazed corner stairwell rises through some five storeys. The name of the architect is not known, but is understood by the present owners to have been European.

The style of the exterior is not, however, continued inside, where the décor is ebullient and sinuous. Bulbous plaster shapes, painted in powder blue and cream, protrude from ceilings and walls, swirl around corners and house concealed lighting. Zigzag panels in similar colours decorate the stairwells. Such decorative features sit rather uncomfortably alongside the austere, dark grey marble floors and long rows of steel-framed windows, prompting the suggestion that the interior decoration is by a different hand.

The intimate auditorium contains 682 seats, cushioned push-backs in the balcony and wooden in the stalls. The small stage has a moulded, flat-topped arched proscenium, but has lost the flanking pilasters and its curtain and the rudimentary back-stage facilities have fallen into disuse. The original, small format screen survives and is still in use.

The highpoint for the Darpana came soon after it opened in 1950, when the cinema was selected to present the Calcutta Première of Chaplin's film *Limelight* and in 1956 the film star Raj Kapoor attended the opening of his expressionist social comedy *Jagte Raho* (aka *Ek Din Raatre* or *Under Cover of Night*), a film by the Bengali actor-director Somblau Mitra. For many years, the Darpana ran programmes of high quality, English and Hindi-language films, but nowadays, it only shows re-issued, Bengali productions from 'Tollywood'.

The cinema is completely unmodernised and has used the same equipment since opening: three Peerless Magnarc projectors with Simplex optics from America and a GEC mono sound system imported from Britain. Although repositioned, the small screen prevents the proper showing of Cinemascope; instead, the film is projected on the standard screen, masked top and bottom to create an elongated format. Unsurprisingly, it attracts very small audiences.

↑ *The screen set up within the original small proscenium and curved stage.*

→ *The Modernist exterior of the Darpana.*

Paradise
Bentick Street

The marble-clad exterior of the Paradise is a chaste Moderne design spoilt by a later, clumsy, over-decorated canopy, whereas the interior is a remarkably extravagant display of Indo-Deco styling. Every available surface is elaborately embellished with moulded, painted or illuminated decoration.

Foyers and stairwells are panelled, mirrored and indirectly lit. The decorative plasterwork of the 1,118-seater auditorium is painted in pastel shades of green, pink and blue depicting flowers and foliage within bold geometric patterns and stripes. Before a performance and in the interval, a huge, recessed light-box in the centre of the ceiling entertains patrons with a light show of ever-changing colours ranging from steely blues to deep reds. Then, as house lights dim and the tasselled curtain starts to rise, the moulded, back-lit proscenium is bathed in a succession of coloured lights beginning with deep violet and running through the spectrum to red, whilst wall sconces and ceiling coves produce additional colourful effects. Only acoustic tiling at the rear of the stalls mars the overall effect. The Paradise was built in c.1958 and is a near-complete survival of contemporary cinema design; its architect, however, has yet to be identified.

↑ *The proscenium lighting display is presented just before a show commences.*

15. Chennai/Madras

Until 1996, Chennai, the capital of the State of Tamil Nadu, was called Madras. Founded in 1639 as a fortified trading post for the British East India Company, it developed into one of the most significant of the Company's settlements. From the original Fort, still largely intact, the city spread south along the coast. A distinguished architectural legacy survives from the colonial era including many buildings in the Indo-Saracenic style and churches bequeathed to the city by Portuguese and Armenian settlers.

Currently, the Chennai metropolitan area, India's fourth largest with a population of some six million, has around sixty cinemas, but, notwithstanding its important cinematic history and reputed obsession with film culture, the theatres themselves are somewhat disappointing. Many of the original large city-centre venues have been demolished and most of those remaining are generally very rundown. In 1999, a local newspaper referred to "... the demise of the theatres in the City ... and the shoddy and the completely degraded state in which many of them are limping on...."

By the end of the 20th century, the city's film production colony nicknamed 'Collywood' had outstripped 'Bollywood' in the number of films produced each year to become the largest in the country; however, being mainly Tamil and Telugu-language films their distribution is more limited.

Gaiety
Harris Road

The Gaiety is one of the first purpose-built cinemas in India. It was opened by the partnership of Raghupathi Venkaiah (?-1941) and his son, Raghupati Surya Prakasha Rao (1901-56), known as Raghupati Surya Prakash. Venkaiah ran a photographic studio in Madras. Around 1910, he started exhibiting programmes of short moving pictures, at first in Madras and later in other cities on the Sub-Continent, using an imported 'Chrono-Megaphone' apparatus in conjunction with a gramophone to provide an embryonic system of synchronised sound. Then, in 1914, with his son he built the Gaiety and later opened two more cinemas in Madras, the Crown and the (demolished) Globe.

During subsequent travels in Europe and America, Prakash studied filmmaking including a visit to F. W. Murnau in Germany. He returned home in 1920 ready to begin film production and in the following year, the family partnership founded the Star of the East Studio, where he established a career as a director. He was subsequently involved with many other production companies including Guarantee Pics, the General Picture Corporation, for which he made the film *Leila the Star of Mingrelia* (1931), Srinivasa Cinetone Studio, Sundraram Sound Studio as well as a number of distribution companies. From the mid-1930s, Prakash operated as a freelance director making Tamil-language films; his reputation rests primarily on his meticulous craftsmanship.

Of the original appearance of the Gaiety, only decorative columns in the foyer apparently survived a comprehensive 1970s remodelling. Although nothing else is visible today, more may remain hidden underneath the later cladding. Ground-floor openings

have been filled in and the two-storey building is now encased in a variety of slabs and cement render: some flat, others with diamond patterns. A crudely superimposed facing, presumably intended as a *chajja*, is fixed above slat-covered first floor windows.

The auditorium is a simple, unadorned rectangular structure under a pitched roof covered with asbestos sheeting. The seating is in a stadium configuration: all wooden, many damaged or entirely removed. Nowadays extremely rundown, the flat-rate admission charge is exceptionally low and the cinema survives by showing X-rated films.

↑ *The exterior of the Gaiety with its uninspiring 1970s remodelling.*

Sri Murugan

St Xavier Street

Built in 1917 as a drama house called the Mercy Theatre, it was converted to a cinema three years later and renamed the Kinema Centre. The current name was adopted in 1960. Apart from a new colourful façade added at that time and technical changes such as new Bauer/Simplex projectors installed in the early 1990s, the cinema is almost unaltered and still uses an old, unnamed mono sound system. The auditorium is a stadium design with 808 wooden seats. In the front they consist of nothing more than long planks of wood fixed together with crude seat dividers; the rear seats are separated by metal standards incorporating a large swastika or sauvastika, an ancient symbol of prosperity in Hindu mythology.

Many famous people, mainly political figures such as Nehru and Subhas Chandra Bose, have attended the Sri Murugan and their visits are recorded in an extensive display of framed photographs in the foyer. Most important, though, was the visit made in 1926 by Mahatma Gandhi. The chair in which he sat is a revered possession and no one has been allowed to use it since.

Nearby is the Prince Theatre. Built by the owner of the Murugan in 1923, it has never been used as a theatre as it has been unable to obtain a license. Nowadays, it houses a plastics factory, but still on the façade pediment is its name and the Prince of Wales's feathers.

↑ The Sri Murugan façade installed in the 1960s.

↑ The owner of the Murugan, V. M. Paramasiva Mudalier, sitting in his office beside the chair that Gandhi used in 1926.

Star Talkies
Quaid-e-Milleth High Road

Of uncertain date and formerly a live drama venue called the Popular Theatre, by the early 1930s it had been converted into a cinema with the name Star Talkies. Originally, entry was through an imposing arch, but this is now disused and superseded by a simple gateway.

Standing in the centre of a large, empty compound is the auditorium hall, with a rendered façade topped by a stepped pediment and prominently displayed star motif. Behind is what appears to be a purely utilitarian building with a corrugated sheet roof; inside, however, both walls and ceiling bear traces of a decorative plasterwork scheme although any evidence of a proscenium or stage facilities has disappeared. The 921 wooden seats are arranged on a single floor. Equipment installed in 1955 is still used: Peerless Magnarc/RCA projectors with two mono sound systems, one RCA the other manufactured locally.

Today the cinema is very rundown and many seats are broken, but in former times the Star was a prestigious venue. Evidence is preserved in the manager's office: two luxurious, cushioned pushbacks removed from the auditorium thirty years ago before the present crude seating was installed.

→ *The shuttered street entrance of the Star – the emblem on the pediment of the auditorium hall is visible above the courtyard wall.*

Crown Talkies
Mint Street

This is the second venue opened by Venkaiah and Prakash in Madras, although information varies as to whether it was a purpose-built cinema or a conversion of an existing live theatre. The date of construction is unknown but it was operating as a cinema called the Crown in 1923, presumably amending the name after the advent of sound. The auditorium hall is at one end of a gated courtyard, its façade surmounted by a Baroque stone pediment. Leading from an open-sided lobby is the foyer, a small room subdivided by painted Corinthian columns which support a classical moulded ceiling. Along each side of the building are verandahs with metalwork screens depicting sunbursts. Inside the single-floor, 1,024-seater auditorium all decoration ceases; this is a purely functional space without a proscenium or any other indication of a theatrical past.

↑ *Crown Talkies – looking through the open-sided lobby towards the auditorium hall.*

Casino
Harris Road

A white marble sculpture of a naked female figure on a rearing horse is the centrepiece of the courtyard in front of the Casino's white Moderne façade. At either side are semi-circular stairwells with elongated fenestration and beyond, verandahs partially enclosed by streamline grilles between columns with grey and red bands. The large foyers are, nowadays, almost unfurnished, but what remains of the original décor is remarkable: modernistic metalwork banisters, amber opalescent light bowls highlighting geometric mouldings in the ceiling and a large mural by C. & Associates of Bombay depicting three languid women resting on a stone wall. Some original windows have recently been replaced by Art Nouveau-style stained glass.

In the auditorium, the 783 all-padded seats are arranged in stalls and a balcony. Moulded plasterwork of circles and horizontal banding decorates the walls and over the proscenium, but acoustic tiles obscure the ceiling. Stylish handrails flank the vomitories and staircases. Most dramatic are two large, square pillars with moulded and illuminated glass capitals supporting the front of the balcony.

Two Gaumont-Kalee (GB Kalee Model 2) projectors have been in use since the cinema opened in 1943. A recently installed DTS Digital Sound system replaces an old Duosonic mono valve amplifier, which is kept in reserve.

↑ *The mural by C. & Associates of Bombay in the balcony foyer.*

← *A detail of the metal banisters enclosing the stairs to the balcony foyer.*

→ *The Casino is at the rear of a large courtyard - in the centre is a sculpture of a female on a rearing horse.*

Sun

(Demolished)

The Sun closed in the early 1990s. The site was cleared to make way for a block of flats - one of many Art Deco super cinemas in Chennai that have been demolished in recent years. (from a photocopy of an unidentified photograph)

Sri Khrishna Talkies
Tiruvothiyur High Road

Above the prominent canopy is a massive, cylindrical, crowned and ribbed tower with a vertical sign rising the full height of the façade. The building is of brick construction under large flat areas of cement render embellished with somewhat chaste Moderne decoration. Pillared verandahs along either side provide access to the auditorium, one side for women with seats inside reserved for their use, the other for men.

Apart from further examples of restrained mouldings and a corner stairwell lit dramatically by a two-storey glass-block window, front of house areas are mostly plain. Overlapping tiers of semi-circular plasterwork mouldings on the walls and a U-shaped coving of classical inspiration on the ceiling decorate what is otherwise a utilitarian auditorium hall. Nevertheless, a serpentine-fronted stage and simple rectangular proscenium are present, without a curtain and lacking any apparent backstage facilities.

Nominally offering 1,208 seats, cushioned in the balcony and plastic in the stalls, well over 200 are damaged beyond use. Equipment installed thirty years ago is still in use: two Westrex 35mm projectors with a mono sound system made by the same firm.

The Chennai architect Munirathnam Naidu designed the Sri Krishna. When opened in 1950, it was considered one of the city's most prestigious picture palaces, but, fifty years on, is very rundown and its future uncertain.

← *The facade of Sri Khrishna Talkies is dominated by the ribbed tower feature and vertical sign.*

Shanti
Anna Salai

The foundation stone was laid in 1959 and the cinema opened in 1961. The Shanti is owned by the Ganesan family, who are involved in many aspects of film-making, distribution and exhibition. A leading member of the family, Viluppuram Chinnaiahpillai Ganesan known as Sivaji Ganesan (b.1927), is one of the biggest Tamil film superstars and photographs of him in some of his many roles are displayed in the foyer. Sivaji has also been a political activist, who at one time or another supported most of the parties in Tamil Nadu State.

↑ *The patriotic message below the curtain is illuminated as the curtain rises for the start of a show.*

← *One of the etched windows in the foyer made by the Rakash Mirror Co. of Bombay and possibly designed by Namjoshi.*

Although named after his daughter Shanti, which means peace, the design of the cinema and its courtyard setting with pond and water lilies is imbued with religious symbolism. The nine planets, twenty-seven stars and sixty-four windows in the façade are all numbers of significance in Hindu iconography. The cinema was designed by the architect and contractor G. Umapathy with interior decoration by W. M. Namjoshi. Extensive lobby and foyer spaces have a unified decorative scheme of swirling plaster mouldings, Moderne metalwork light-boxes and etched glass made by the Rakash Mirror Co. of Bombay. One panel depicts a naked female figure holding aloft a bowl spouting water.

The 1,224-seat auditorium is on two levels of stalls and a balcony. Walls and ceiling are embellished with overlapping plasterwork panels ending in exaggerated scrolls. The elaborate proscenium is made up of fluted plasterwork columns within a canted and moulded frame. A political message - "Long Live the Republic of India" - is printed in big letters below the screen. In the projection box are two Westrex-14/Simplex XL projectors made in India and a DTS sound system.

Plans have been drawn up by the Kansas City architect Theodore Knapp to turn the cinema into a multi-screen venue, initially creating two new smaller auditoria with others to follow later. Whilst retaining the exterior of the building, all internal decoration will be lost.

↑ *Sivaji Ganesan in one of his many film roles on display in the foyer.*

Devi

Anna Salai

Within the headquarters office block of the film equipment, distribution and exhibition conglomerate TNK Cinemas Ltd is the first five-screen multiplex built in India. The design of both the building and the cinemas was undertaken by the firm's own in-house architects.

The first auditorium, the Devi with 1,032 seats opened in 1971. Four others followed over a period of fifteen years: the Devi Paradise with 1,212 seats, the Devi Bala with 366 seats, the Devi Kala with 303 seats and the Devi Miniature with 60/70 seats available only for private hire. The two largest screens are equipped with 70mm and Dolby sound, the others have 35mm, one with a DTS system and the remainder with ordinary stereo sound.

Notwithstanding a somewhat grim, institutional air about the common front of house facilities, the building is fully air-conditioned and the cinemas themselves luxuriously fitted. However, decoration is minimal. The Devi complex website offers computerised booking, film reviews, fan clubs, chat lines and all the other requisites for online living. As a marketing device, large colourful tickets are issued which can be retained as a memento of the cinema visit.

← The name of the second cinema to open at the complex, Devi Paradise, is prominently displayed on the roof of the office block.

16. Delhi

Delhi is the architectural non-pareil of Indian cities. Its significance to Indian history lies in its strategic position: standing at the narrowest point between the Himalayas and the Arvalli hills, thereby in command of the route from the North West frontier to the fertile plains of the South.

Old Delhi, encompassing seven earlier cities and sometimes described as the 'Seven Cities', is the site of the Mughal emperors' capital and their palace in the Red Fort (1639-48). Nowadays, Old Delhi is a crowded metropolis of bazaars and factories, interspersed by ancient mosques and tombs of exquisite craftsmanship.

New Delhi - the Eighth Delhi – declared the capital of India in 1911 is at its heart a triumphalist Imperial city created by the British to the designs of Sir Edwin Lutyens and Sir Herbert Baker. Completed by 1931, yet within twenty years the British Emperor, like his Mughal predecessors, had vanished into history leaving the newly independent country with a capital whose public buildings display a grandeur scarcely equalled anywhere in the world.

The range and quality of the buildings erected in New Delhi since Independence is also remarkable, with cinemas ranked highly among these developments. Although several older theatres in the City Centre have closed recently, some to make way for stations on the new Metro railway, approximately sixty venues are still operating within the Greater Delhi area for a population nowadays in excess of thirteen million.

Excelsior
Lal Kuan Street
Old Delhi

The Excelsior has an inconspicuous frontage, no wider than one of the adjacent small shops. Until converted into a cinema in 1934, the building, which dates from the 19th century, was a live drama theatre and reputedly the oldest surviving venue in the city. Apart from the introduction of the cinema equipment, little else has changed. It is owned by the Chitnis family, who also own another Delhi cinema, West End Talkies.

A tiny, square foyer is entered straight off the street and beyond this the building widens slightly to accommodate the small auditorium with 489 seats on two levels; wooden tip-ups in the stalls, cushioned in the balcony. The ceiling has acoustic tile cladding, but elsewhere the walls and proscenium display their original classical mouldings. Currently, every surface is painted in vibrant reds, blues and yellows with the mouldings picked out in contrasting colours. A deep red drop curtain is still in use.

The projection box has Bauers installed in the 1960s and an ancient Motograph projector still in working order. Sound is provided by a Klangfilm mono sound system. One of the staff, aged over eighty, has been working here as a projectionist for more than 55 years. *(illustrated on page 51)* The cinema is a second-run house, showing X-rated adult and crime movies. Seat prices are exceptionally low as it caters primarily for a poor working-class audience.

← The Excelsior is situated in one of busiest streets in Old Delhi - the jumble of electrical wiring on the street standard is a common sight.

Robin

Ghanta Ghar Chowk
Old Delhi

Only the vertical sign displaying the name of the cinema and the small entablature behind it give this venue any significant street presence as the entrance itself is extremely narrow and inconspicuous. This building probably started as a live theatre in the late nineteenth or early twentieth century before being adapted in the mid-1930s for full-time cinema use. A long exterior passage serves as an entrance lobby, leading to a small foyer in the auditorium building located behind adjacent shops.

The foyer and stairs have Art Deco details superimposed on the older fabric and a large stepped mirror decorates the stairs up the balcony. The walls in the auditorium display an array of stripped classical features: shallow moulded panels, pilasters and niches and a proscenium of deeply ribbed teak, but the more recent, coved ceiling has bold patterns of Art Deco zigzag mouldings. The drop curtain is still in use. The Robin accommodates 512 in fixed wooden seats in the stalls and fixed cushioned ones in a single box and gallery-like balcony. In the projection box are Photophone 35 Continentals with Photophone Hi-Lites made in India and mono Photophone Melody 60 sound.

↑ *The classically-inspired decoration in the auditorium.*

← *The sign and entablature of the Robin.*

Regal

Indira Chowk, Connaught Place
New Delhi

The Regal was built and owned by the developer and contractor Sir Sobha Singh. It was the first cinema to be constructed in New Delhi, situated on the perimeter of Connaught Place in what is now the most popular retail centre of the city. However, in 1932 when the cinema opened, this area had yet to develop commercially and the Regal was apparently not an immediate success. As Robert Grant Irving notes:

> A solitary theatre, the Regal Cinema, seemed but the newest of Delhi's countless mausolea, often with less than a half-dozen patrons, whom the proprietors begged to accept a refund and leave.[20]

Once Connaught Place was established as a prestigious location, the Regal soon became a fashionable place of entertainment with direct access from the exclusive Davicos (now Standard) Restaurant located on the first floor of the building. In the *Screen Supplement* issued to celebrate the Regal's Golden Jubilee, the owner Rajeshwar Dayal recalled:

> When the Viceroy or Governor-General visited the theatre, a red carpet was laid from the porch down to the foyer and up to the boxes. A thick maroon velvet curtain adorned the stage.....The patrons were mostly British and Americans when the war broke out (and) they were very orderly and disciplined. Even high (ranking) officers would stand in the queue to purchase tickets.[21]

Dayal's management commenced in 1938 and for the first ten years the cinema screened only English-language films. In December 1940, The Viceroy, Lord Linlithgow, attended the Indian Premiere of *Gone With the Wind* but during the Second World War, the cinema was frequently requisitioned by the army for military briefings, putting the entire building 'out of bounds'. Until Independence, the Regal also presented stage shows and numerous visiting British repertory companies presented Shakespeare and other classics. Noel Coward performed here, when he was a guest of the Viceroy, Lord Mountbatten.

After Independence, both Hindi and English films were shown but it remained a premier first-run house exhibiting many Disney and Rank productions. In 1954, with the screening of *The Robe*, it became the first cinema in North India to show a Cinemascope film. The Prime Minster, Jawaharlal Nehru, together with other members of his cabinet, was in the audience on the First Night. The cinema also had a policy of showing art-house films, including filmed versions of Shakespeare and other classics. Satyajit Ray films were a regular feature and many productions from the Soviet Union were given their Indian premiere here.

The Regal was designed in 1930-32 by Walter Sykes George (1881-1962) in his favoured classical style. George had been in Delhi since 1915, initially as Herbert Baker's representative and in 1920 established his own practice in the city. He was responsible for a number of important buildings in New Delhi, most notably St Thomas's Church (1932) and alterations to St Stephen's College (1938). After Independence he stayed on in India, becoming Principal of the Delhi School of

↑ *Rajeshwar Dayal (photographed in 1988)*

→ *The exterior of the Regal.*

Architecture and was elected President of both the Indian Institute of Architects and the Institute of Town Planning. In 1962, he was awarded the C.B.E. Summarizing his achievements, the American architectural historian Peter Serenyi wrote:

> Walter George's handling of detail and building materials, his sensitivity to function and climate, and his attentiveness to scale and context contributed to his becoming the most influential younger member of the original Lutyens team.[22]

The symmetrical, cement-rendered façade of the Regal has the name of the venue in cutout lettering in the cornice. An arched *porte-cochère* stretches the full width of the frontage, but later this vehicular access was incorporated into the surrounding pavement. Doors open into a pillared and arched, Italianate lobby. This leads into a rectangular foyer with a black and white marble chequerboard floor. Marble stairs ascend through a ribbed arch to an ambulatory curving around the rear of the auditorium. During renovation work in 1955, the walls of the front of house areas were embellished with fine teak panelling, but the original marble pay boxes in the lobby were replaced by new plain ones outside.

The foyer ceiling was subsequently given an unsympathetic, concertina-like cladding. Cinemascope was installed at the same time. To accommodate the new format, the original screen, proscenium and three sets of curtains were removed. The stage area was enlarged to the full width of the auditorium, with the wide screen set between deep white embrasures. The remainder of the small and intimate auditorium, whose walls taper sharply towards the screen, was not altered. Along both sides and across the rear is a continuous arcade of white classical pillars and arches, with a few empty niches above. Painted reliefs depicting idealised landscapes are visible between the side arches. The rear arches, which support the sweeping front wall of the tiny balcony, form a row of small private boxes, each with a pair of free-standing armchairs. Elsewhere, the original tip-up seats remain although somewhat battered, but their number has been slightly reduced to 694. In the projection box are two Magnivox projectors from Chicago, two Westrex Hi-Lite 130s with Westrex-100 stereo sound, a disused 1930s Peerless Kalee and an old Westrex mono system in reserve.

↑ *The Regal auditorium with the row of small arched boxes under the balcony.*

↑↑ *Advertisements for Regal presentations in 1940* (left) *and 1954.*

Odeon

Rajiv Chowk, Connaught Place
New Delhi

The Odeon is situated within the colossal town-planning scheme at Connaught Place, which commemorates the Duke of Connaught's visit to India in 1921. The outline proposal for a grand plaza was prepared in 1917 by W. H. Nichols, an architect member of the Imperial Delhi Committee. After a number of delays and modifications, Robert Tor Russell produced a plan consisting of three vast, concentric circles of neo-classical terraces around a large park, but lack of commercial interest forced the designs to be reduced from three storeys to two. The colonnaded development, constructed of brick with cement rendering, took from 1928 to 1934 to complete. Designated for retail and entertainment use, the area only slowly established itself as a superior location to the upmarket Chandi Chowk in the Old City.

Robert Tor Russell (1888-1972) entered Government Service in 1914. Upon his appointment as Chief Architect to the Government of India in 1919 until his retirement in 1939, he was responsible for all Government buildings throughout India. Besides Connaught Place, Russell's major achievement in New Delhi is the monumental Eastern and Western Courts facing Janpath.

The exterior of the cinema conformed to the classical design of its neighbours, with paired columns and a moulded entablature. Whether Russell played any part in the interior design of the cinema is not known, but it had an unusual elliptical auditorium with a single rake layout seating approximately 500. Until the Second World War, the cinema was owned by an Italian businessman, but at the outbreak of hostilities he was interned and the Manager, a German, fled the country.

The family firm of Isherdas Sahni & Bros. operated a chain of some twenty cinemas in what after Partition became part of Pakistan. Forced to sell those cinemas, the family moved to Delhi in 1950, purchasing the Odeon in the same year and some time later the nearby Rivoli. In 1960, a decision was taken to upgrade the cinema and the owners engaged the New Delhi architects Master, Sathe & Kothari Associates. The modernised venue re-opened in 1963 with Howard Hawks' safari adventure *Hatari*, starring John Wayne.

Much of the Russell building remained, but so extensively altered or obscured as to destroy most of its value as part of the Connaught Place townscape. All traces of the original entrance, lobby and foyer were removed and a large slab erected in front of the columns of the first-floor façade. The then relatively unknown artist and sculptor Satish Gujral (b.1925) was commissioned to produce a ceramic mosaic for the slab. This now dominates the exterior: his design consists of small brightly coloured tiles set in a pattern of squares, with a number of indentations and projections providing additional interest. This work helped to secure Gujral's reputation and he has since become a hugely successful artist and architect. However, a contemporary review[23] questioned the wisdom of allowing an artist so much aesthetic control, but after disparaging the mosaic "...as a whole, in terms of colour, it gives the feeling of a garment prepared from the leftovers of knitting wool," the architects were praised for their boldness:

> A word of congratulation must go to the municipality who have authorised the cantilevered canopy

↑ Isherdas Sahni (photographed in 1963)

over the entrance. Unless (they) move with the times, living communities must suffer inconvenience because of artistic notions of the dead. To force forty-year old Connaught Circus facades on contemporary buildings like cinema theatres will represent municipal mental slavery and nothing else.

Whatever the intrinsic qualities of Gujral's ceramic design, it is incongruous alongside Russell's classicism. Even more unsettling are the still visible corner sections of the original façade left untouched either side of the artwork with the old vertical Odeon signs in place between Russell's columns. *(illustrated on page 27)* Entry to the cinema is through a long row of glazed, steel doors set back under the thin steel-framed canopy running across the width of the building. The doormats have the cinema's name woven into their design and attendants' uniforms are embroidered with the name on the breast pocket. *(illustrated on frontispiece)* Gujral created more ceramic designs for the walls and stairways in the lobby, here using freer forms to suggest the various processes of filmmaking. Most impressive of the new work is the foyer, which has a dramatic false ceiling of recessed box-like shapes and concealed lighting.

In the auditorium, the rear section of the ellipse was retained, but elsewhere all other original features were removed when the proscenium end was widened to accommodate a new 70mm screen. Surrounded by huge white embrasures without masking or curtains, this fills one entire wall. The remaining curved side and rear walls, however, are a painted trompe d'oeil design in muted colours of what appears to be three-

dimensional triangular patterns; the contemporary review called it "Mexican". The ceiling, covered with tiny pinpoint lights - like stars in a night sky - and plastic light fittings suggesting flying saucers is now something of a space age period piece. A new cantilevered balcony was inserted, enabling the seating capacity to be increased to 854, all pushbacks. At the same time, the projection cabin was raised and re-equipped with two Photophones made in Japan c.1964, an Arco Tau from Italy (made by Microtecnica of Turin) and Indian-manufactured Ultra Stereo; the old RCA system was retained as backup.

↑ *The space age ceiling of stars, a comet and flying saucer shaped lights in the auditorium. On the rear elliptical wall is the "Mexican" trompe d'oeil decoration.*

← *The exterior of the Odeon with Satish Gujral's ceramic design set in front of Robert Tor Russell's classical façade.*

Plaza

Radial Road, Connaught Place
New Delhi

The Plaza opened in 1933. The original classical façade of Robert Tor Russell's Connaught Place building was entered through a central doorway under a small rectangular canopy and the name of the cinema in large neon letters was displayed on the cornice. All this was obliterated when the present unsympathetic slab replacement was built in 1967, but the original design is still apparent in the buildings either side of the cinema. At the same time, the interior was completely renewed and nothing of the earlier decorative scheme remains visible. The foyers are now expensively furnished, but plainly functional spaces with tiled chequerboard floors and marble cladding on the walls. The name of the venue is woven into several large mats. The auditorium with 877 seats in stalls and a balcony is dismal, entirely clad with a crude, peg-board sound insulation and the giant, floating screen is installed in front of bald, white embrasures. Whether any original decoration remains underneath is uncertain. The projection box is equipped for 70mm using two adapted Photophone 16Cs and an Ashcroft Suprex c.1960 with Dolby sound. Eagle Films owns this cinema and the Minerva in Mumbai.

↑ *Early morning sunlight on the exterior of the Plaza. The 1960s slab frontage and steel canopy obscures most of Russell's original building - still partially visible at the left hand corner.*

Golcha

Netaji Subhash Marg
Darya Ganj
New Delhi

Large cutout letters at roof level and a bold vertical sign advertise the cinema, giving the building, whose cement-rendered façade is painted a startling pink, a considerably greater prominence than suggested by its relatively small size. Nowadays, attraction posters fixed on a temporary-looking hoarding obscure part of the upper façade. Under the thin canopy, a row of glazed doors surrounded by marble cladding provides access to the elegant lobby and ticket offices of carved marble and moulded wood.

Once inside, patrons are engulfed in a fantasy of flamboyant, decorative plasterwork, marble cladding, inlaid wood panelling, mirrors and concealed lighting effects, the work of the designer W. M. Namjoshi. The foyers and soda fountain are timber panelled and mirrored with soft cove lighting in swirling ceiling mouldings. An etched glass, designed by the Divecha Glass Works of Bombay, depicts Lord Krishna. Built-in banquette seating has exaggerated, fan-shaped wooden arms.

A more spectacular sight awaits those ascending to balcony level. From the marble-faced lobby, doors open to reveal an enclosed and darkened space of stepped plaster coves, mirrors and concealed lighting effects. Here, a glittering staircase with illuminated, etched glass banisters supporting handrails of glowing red and black rises to the upper foyer, from where a central vomitory provides access to the balcony. All this is a fitting introduction for the auditorium; an Art Deco extravaganza of neo-classical inspiration. Above a reeded wood dado along both sides, moulded pilasters, with metalwork embellishments imitating tiers of temple bells, are illuminated in soft shades of orange and pink light. *(illustrated on page 34)* On the ceiling, scalloped coves descend in overlapping steps towards the screen, where a backlit moulding surrounds the simple rectangular proscenium.

The cinema is air-conditioned and luxurious. The foyers and auditorium are furnished with fitted carpets and all 715 seats in the stalls and balcony are padded pushbacks. Remarkably, the Manager's office is unaltered: a compact wood-panelled room with fitted streamline desk and sofa. This is a period piece, an echo of a cabin aboard a 1930s ocean liner. Even the conveniences have not escaped decoration; the Gents with inlaid woods and etched glass door and the Ladies has columnar torchères flanking its door of mirror quarries. Decoratively, little has changed; the main innovations have lain with the technical equipment.

← *The exterior of the Golcha in eye-catching pink marble cladding and colour washed rendering.*

When Cinemascope was introduced in 1981, the proscenium was extended to accommodate the wider screen. Whilst, apparently, retaining the original design, the new proportions are awkward and the curtains were not replaced. The projection box has Indian-made Cinécita 35mm equipment. Dolby sound was introduced in 1997; an old 4-track Westrex system is kept in reserve. The cinema employs a staff of fifty-six, those at front of house are uniformed.

The Golcha was opened on 12th December 1954 by the Vice-President of India, Dr S. Radhakrishnan. It bears the family name of its founders, the Golcha Group.

← *The illuminated staircase leading to the balcony foyer.*

→ *The auditorium with its flaring yellow and orange recessed lighting behind reeded coves decorated with stylised temple bells.*

→ *The lobby with internal ticket offices.*

New Filmistan

Rani Jhansi Road
New Delhi

Following the enormous box-office success of their Bombay Talkies' film *Kismet* (1943), a re-make of John Cromwell's *Algiers*, the producer Shashadhar Mukherji and director Gyan Mukherji left that studio to set up their own production company, Filmistan, with the film composer Kohli Madan Mohan. Early successes included a number of psychological melodramas reminiscent of the Warner Bros. style, including a couple of films dealing with the 'Quit India' movement. After Independence, Filmistan Studios developed into a big Hollywood-style operation, retaining the services of a large number of writers, actors and directors and its standardised output, mostly a succession of popular musical comedy films, eventually attracted the sobriquet 'Bombay Formula'.

Designed as an outlet for its own productions, in 1957 the studio opened its one and only cinema, the Filmistan in Delhi. The bold Moderne façade has a decorative corner tower with horizontal fins and a superimposed swirling motif, surmounted by the name of the cinema in neon lettering. Pay boxes are sited in the lobby, which leads into a large foyer; the floor and walls marble-clad, the walls with raised mouldings and the ceiling decorated with swirling amoebic-shaped lighting recesses. Stairs to the balcony foyer and café are lit by an impressive double height, glass-block window.

Access to the auditorium, which seats 854 on two levels, is through streamline wooden doors to the stalls and deep, panelled vomitories at balcony level. The auditorium walls and ceiling are decorated with wavy plasterwork mouldings. An elaborate proscenium, with strange, ear-like lobes at the top corners, survived unscathed the introduction of Cinemascope in 1978. The projection box still uses its two original Westrex/Century 35mm projectors with upgraded optics and a recently installed Dolby sound system.

The Filmistan was designed by the prolific Delhi-based firm of Master, Sathe & Kothari Associates, a practice formed by the architects Chimanlal Motilal Master, Laxaman Vishnu Sathe and Naren Kureji Kothari, whose output as well as cinemas – they had earlier revamped the Odeon, New Delhi - includes many other buildings types, especially offices and apartment blocks.

The cinema was not built in a fashionable district, but in a working class neighbourhood 'on the wrong side of the tracks'. Workers from nearby factories made up the bulk of its audience, but these local patrons were lost once businesses closed or relocated to new suburban premises and as a result box-office receipts declined during the 1990s and it became rundown. However, a recent refurbishment has included technical improvements, new seats and most obviously, a new colour scheme. Inside this has involved highlighting plaster mouldings in bright pastel colours; outside, the original white rendered façade has been repainted in a garish display of orange and royal blue. Upon re-opening in 2000, the name was changed to New Filmistan.

← *The New Filmistan in its new, bright orange and blue livery.*

Shiela

D B Gupta Road, Pahar Ganj
New Delhi

You could say I'm about the best man in my field, but then it's a very limited field.[24]

The words are those of Ben Schlanger (1904-1971), speaking in 1966 whilst working on the completion of the Sydney Opera House after Jørn Utzon's departure. Seven years earlier in 1959, he had been commissioned to design this cinema by its founder, D. C. Kaushish, who was determined to build a state-of-the-art auditorium taking full advantage of the recent developments in exhibition technology.

A cinema had been planned for this site as long ago as 1937, but no construction took place until the late 1950s, when work began on Schlanger's scheme, with the Delhi-based practice Master, Sathe & Kothari Associates as local Supervising Architects. Construction was overseen by A. Ajit Singh and B. A. Mistry and the International Talkie Equipment Co. was responsible for the sound and projection installation. Seating was supplied by 20th Century-Fox. The cinema is named after the owner's wife; to ensure that this remained a secret until the opening ceremony, the façade was hidden behind tarpaulins during construction. Initially called Shiela Theatre 70, this was later shortened to Shiela. Opening on 12th January 1961, it was the first cinema in India to be equipped with 70mm – the facade advertises this technological development with a huge representation of a wide curving screen in concrete.

The stalls foyer is located beneath the balcony seating ramp, whose exposed soffit forms a dramatic stepped ceiling supported on massive concrete struts. Set above the entrance lobby, the balcony foyer is an open gallery space enclosed by thin metal railing overlooking the stalls foyer. Here, the cylindrical, exposed concrete columns have been boxed in with mirror panels and attraction displays and the original Charles Eames metal chairs removed. Elsewhere, nothing significant has been changed; the exposed concrete scheme is relieved only by an assertive 20-metre long abstract mural, the work of the French artist Luc Durand. Originally commissioned for the auditorium, an alternative position was found in the stalls foyer after Schlanger's refusal to countenance such a proposal. It extends the full width of one wall, continuing behind the row of concrete struts and running uninterrupted over three pairs of auditorium doors.

In compliance with Schlanger's theories, the auditorium has no applied decoration; rather it is a satisfyingly calm, almost mesmeric space, illuminated by deep blue light. The walls are clad with grey, textured panels, the ceiling somewhat darker. The huge screen fills the 'fourth wall' just as Schlanger planned, without either masking or a dark surround, although the original screen has since been replaced by one with a 6-metre deep curve - here called *Shielarama*. The seating comprises 1,020 luxurious, cushioned pushbacks, which in the stalls are set on a double rake; the rear half on a conventional incline towards the screen, the front half on a reverse incline.

In the projection box are three 70/35mm Ashcroft Super Cinexs with Bauer U2 optics from Germany, two Photophones (which are not used) and a Dolby sound system. The staff numbers more than seventy; those in front of house are uniformed and accommodation for some, including families, is provided within the building. At

→ *The white-painted concrete representation of a 70mm screen dominates the façade of the Shiela.*

the rear of the auditorium a spiral staircase leads to a row of flats behind a passage screened by concrete *jalis*.

The inaugural presentation was 20th Century-Fox's *Solomon & Sheba*. During the first fifteen years, the cinema ran only English-language films and built up a close relationship with the big Hollywood Studios. Jack Valenti, David Lean and, for the Indian Premiere of her film *Barbarella*, Jane Fonda made appearances at the cinema. Since 1975, the programming policy has adapted to reflect changing audience tastes. It now shows fewer foreign films, whilst gradually increasing the number of 'Bollywood' productions.

The Shiela is an important work by an architect described by a writer in the *Theatre Catalog*[25] as one of the most influential of the 20th century working in the field of theatre design. Many improvements resulted from research carried out by Ben Schlanger; most importantly developments in illumination, acoustics and reduced floor rakes.

Whilst accepting decorative ornamentation elsewhere in the theatre, he rejected such an approach in the auditorium which he believed should be planned solely for the acoustical, visual and psychological requirements necessary to provide a suitable setting for an audience to view a motion picture. During his long career Schlanger designed or was the consultant responsible for hundreds of theatres and other auditoria all over the world. Besides the already mentioned Sydney Opera House, Schlanger's best-known commission is the General Assembly hall of the United Nations Headquarters in New York, for which he was one of a team of consultants. Summarising his career and achievements, the article in the *Theatre Catalog* concludes:

> Schlanger saw that his plan to subordinate everything in the auditorium in order to focus all of the audience attention to the screen was not yet (in the 1930s) to be appreciated by the exhibitors. Thoroughly convinced that he was right, Schlanger continued to fight for the construction of simplified auditoria. A look at many of the recently erected theatres will offer proof that this battle was not a futile one. Today the neutralised auditorium setting for motion picture projection has been recognised and accepted all over the world.

← *Ben Schlanger with the Mayor of Delhi and the owner of the Shiela, D. C. Kaushish (right), at a reception given in his honour.*

→ *The mural by Luc Durand extends the full width of the stalls foyer between the concrete struts which support the balcony ramp.*

→ *The view of the screen from the stalls - before a show begins the entire auditorium is bathed in deep blue light.*

India International Centre

Max Muller Marg
Lodhi Estate
New Delhi

At the Lodi Estate, adjacent to the famous Gardens and 16th-century tombs, the American-born architect Joseph Allen Stein (b.1912) designed a series of buildings for major institutional clients. The buildings form a harmonious group, each different in design but employing a similar architectural vocabulary: an attempt, the architect later explained, to integrate the urban and the pastoral.

Stein was born in Omaha, Nebraska. He worked in the office of Richard Neutra in Los Angeles and later independently in San Francisco before moving to India in 1952 to accept the Directorship of the School of Architecture in Calcutta, a post Neutra was instrumental in obtaining for him. In 1955, he moved to New Delhi, where he continues to practice. In Post-Independence India, Stein found a political situation congenial with his social idealism and where he was able to develop his then prescient ideas on ecology and environmental sustainability. Over the next half-century, collaborating with many other designers, he has been responsible for a large body of work across the Sub-Continent.

The India International Centre was founded in the late 1950s by Dr S. Radhakrishnan, the Vice-President of India, and John D. Rockefeller III, the Rockefeller Foundation providing substantial funding. It was opened by Dr Radhakrishnan on 22nd January 1962. As well as being a cultural and social centre, the I. I. C. provides the facilities of a private club and hotel for members. Designed as a series of landscaped courts connected by shaded walkways, the buildings are constructed using an in-situ reinforced concrete frame with load-bearing infil walls of local grey stone worked on site using traditional, low-technology, labour intensive techniques.

One of the main blocks of the development terminates with the hexagonal auditorium. Inside, exposed stone walls support a low domical roof; its pre-cast concrete Y-shaped structural elements forming a shell-like honeycomb ceiling. This characteristic Stein feature was designed with the structural engineer Vishnu Joshi. Planned as a multi-purpose space, the auditorium has a small stage without a proscenium and minimal back-stage facilities. Used principally for seminars during the day, it runs programmes of art-house, archive and foreign-language films at evening shows. When not in use, the upstage Cinemascope screen is masked by curtains. The projection box, which was originally a small lecture room and only later adapted for its current use, has Cinesales Xenon LH3 35mm projectors and stereo sound system. DVD and laser disc facilities are also available. The auditorium accommodates 240 in wide, steeply raked stalls and a small balcony.

In an interview, his one time partner, the architect Balkrishna Doshi, commented on Stein's achievement:

> There is no-one's work in India which is as meticulously done, or as well-built,....well-designed and appropriate. This is a great contribution, because if you look around India over the last thirty years, other buildings haven't stood the test of time – in terms of finish, in terms of their quality, in terms of construction – even in terms of aesthetics, whilst his have.[26]

← *The main group of buildings of the Centre – the auditorium building is on the left..*

← *The auditorium - set up for a daytime seminar*

Shri Ram Centre for the Performing Arts

Safdar Hashmi Marg
New Delhi

The architect Charles Correa wrote of Shiv Nath Prasad (b.1922), the designer of the Shri Ram Centre:

> Prasad has never been anywhere near Le Corbusier. He seems to have picked up the idiom by a process of osmosis. But he has mastered more than just the vocabulary; in all his work there is a poetic impulse which would do credit to the guru himself. He works with one or two assistants and makes all the drawings (including the detailed working drawing) himself. His output is really as personal a product as a piece of handicraft or handloom.[27]

Built between 1966 and 1969 on a small, city-centre site near other cultural institutions, the Centre is named after Bharat Ram, the founder of a private trust specialising in the promotion of dance, drama and music. A two-storey, cylindrical structure is occupied by front of house areas on the ground floor and an auditorium on the first floor. The square, cantilevered block above originally contained a small auditorium designed for film and puppet shows, a rehearsal space and lodging for visiting companies. This floor is now leased out as revenue earning office space and a second small auditorium has been opened in the basement. Later, an annexe, designed by the architects Kanvinde, Rai & Chowdhury, was added at the rear of the main building to accommodate a library, office and rehearsal area.

The building is constructed of *in-situ* reinforced concrete with exposed shuttering marks. The ground floor foyer is dominated by a 'ceiling' of massive radial beams cantilevered from concrete columns, which support the circular auditorium above. Here, 600 seats are set around the performance area or screen in a steeply raked arc, with a small balcony wrapped around at the rear. Walls are partially clad with timber battens and the ceiling is of a pronounced egg-crate design, both finishes planned by the architect for acoustic enhancement.

For a multi-purpose space used by diverse outside organisations, arts groups and production companies, the facilities are designed to be as flexible as possible. The stage is adaptable for either thrust or proscenium style performance. When used as a cinema, the screen is flown in upstage from the fly tower, which rises into the square office floor above. Lighting is at the discretion of the hiring company, controlled, together with the permanent sound system, from a box at the rear of the balcony. This is also the projection cabin for film shows; its equipment is currently limited to 16mm but this is to be upgraded for laser disc and video presentations.

The Shri Ram Centre is not a subsidised arts facility, but run as a commercial operation. Although performances of classical Indian music and Hindu musical and dance dramas form the bulk of its programmes, the hall also accommodates film shows, particularly documentaries, arts presentations and art-house productions.

Prasad was responsible for other important buildings in New Delhi including the Akbar Hotel (1965-69) and the Institute of Chartered Accountants (1971). A remarkable cinema he designed in the early 1960s never got beyond the foundation stage. *(illustrated on page 42)*

→ *The Shri Ram Centre. The auditorium is housed in the upper section of the drum just below the projecting top office floor.*

Chanakya

Chanakyapuri
New Delhi

The Chanakya was planned as part of a large, official scheme comprising a cultural centre, shops and an hotel on a Government-owned site in Chanakyapuri, an enclave in New Delhi's exclusive diplomatic sector. The name honours an eminent diplomat who served a 3rd century B.C. Maurian emperor. Construction work began in 1969 and was completed by April of the following year. The inauguration ceremony, which was performed by Admiral Nanda, Chief of Naval Staff, did not take place until later that year on 17th December, the event receiving national news coverage. The Raj Kapoor film *Mera Naam Joker (My Name is Joker)* was the first presentation.

The cinema was leased to Aditya Khanna, an established exhibitor and owner of Khanna Talkies in Old Delhi, and is now managed by his son. Designed from the outset as a prestigious venue, it has hosted innumerable premieres, special screenings, lectures and other cultural events and is a principal venue for New Delhi film festivals. Many Heads of State, ambassadors and other VIPs have visited this theatre and the filmmakers James Ivory and Ismail Merchant attended the World Premieres of their productions *Heat & Dust* in 1982 and *A Passage to India* in 1984. David Lean was a frequent visitor and a memorial season of his films was a sell-out.

Regular patrons come mostly from the surrounding diplomatic corps and wealthy, car-owing Dilliwalas, the cinema being in a somewhat inaccessible area not served by public transport. During the first twenty years or so, this was a favourite haunt of Delhi's young jet set, but such a trendy atmosphere reputedly deterred older patrons. Once fashion changed and this group moved elsewhere, the management deliberately cultivated a more permanent, upper middle-class, family audience.

Seat prices are high, reflecting its exclusive location and select clientele. Staff number over one hundred and thirty. When the cinema opened, it presented first-run Hindi films and a few English-language productions. Later, this policy changed and it now programmes only high quality English-language films and the occasional Indian art-house production.

The Chanakya project was awarded to the Delhi architect Prakash Narain Mathur (b.1930), in association with Rajinder Singh and Satish Davar, with K A. Patel the official Government Engineer. It is Mathur's only theatre project to date. Of exposed reinforced concrete construction, the exterior surfaces appear a sober grey in shadow and a glowing honey colour in sunlight. The bulky mass of the windowless auditorium, raised high off the ground above the partially glazed ground floor pay boxes, foyers and offices, is supported on splayed struts, which also anchor the steel cables attached to the ends of concrete beams spanning the roof. The only applied decoration is an abstract sheet steel and wire sculpture on the wall above the main entrance doors and a large blue neon name sign on the roof. The internal layout of the building, the shape of the auditorium and its seating ramp descending towards a huge screen wall are clearly discernible in the external form of the structure. Set back from the road behind a lushly planted garden containing two large square pools with fountains, it presents no façade to the street: the pay boxes and entrance along one side face towards the car parking areas at the rear of the plot.

← *The shape of the auditorium is apparent in the Chanakya's dramatic exterior form.*

Entry is through glazed, polished metal doors directly into a large open foyer space, without a lobby. Stairs lead up to a long refreshment bar on one side and to the auditorium on the other. Floors and stair treads are dark grey polished marble, the walls and ceilings mostly a light coloured, smooth concrete, except for some stairwells painted blue or clad with orange tiles.

The design of the vast auditorium is unusual. Front and central stalls are set on shallow rakes, whilst either side and across the rear, steep ramps form what in effect are two wide, stepped slips and a balcony. Ribbed wooden dados and dark, acoustic fibre panels fill the wall spaces between paired, exposed concrete columns, which connect to similar roof beams whose extremities split into Vs, laterally subdividing the enormous expanse of ceiling. Large, illuminated, sans-serif lettering indicates the exits. The floor is thickly carpeted and all 1,096 seats are luxurious pushbacks. Colour is confined to muted browns and buffs. The 24-metre-wide floating screen has no surround and is positioned for a zero-degree throw from a projection box situated at the rear of the stalls. It is equipped for 70mm and Dolby sound.

Delhi's extreme climate has exacerbated maintenance problems; nowadays, the deteriorating concrete requires a near-continuous programme of repairs and although recognised as one of Delhi's modern landmarks it does not qualify currently for statutory protection

← *Two views showing the exterior structure of the rear balcony. The restaurant and foyers are tucked in underneath.*

→ *The auditorium from the rear of the balcony.*

Shakuntalam

Pragati Maidan
Permanent Exhibition Complex
New Delhi

The 1972 National Trade Fair was planned to mark the 25th Anniversary of Indian Independence. After winning the architectural competition, the Delhi-based architect Raj Rewel (b.1934) was awarded the commission. His initial proposal to use prefabricated elements proved too costly and Rewel was forced to adopt a solution employing the most basic and labour-intensive (but relatively economical) methods of on-site reinforced concrete construction. The resulting crudely finished, poured concrete surfaces actually enhance the sculptural qualities of the extraordinary structures conceived by the architect.

Situated in a prominent location between India Gate and the Yamuna River, the permanent complex includes five massive exhibition halls displaying India's industrial and technological achievements, surrounded by restaurants and entertainment venues. Subsequent individual State pavilions built around the site are in a bewildering variety of styles.

The centrepiece of the Pragati Maidan is a concourse around which Rewel has placed the great honeycomb-like exhibition halls, amphitheatre and a low block-like structure housing the Shakuntalam and Falaknuma Theatres. The entrance for the Shakuntalam, a conventional multi-purpose auditorium, is tucked away at the side of a vast flight of steps up to the Falaknuma, a 400-seat open-air theatre built on its roof. Whereas this is used for dance and musical productions, apart from special presentations or trade shows during exhibition periods, the Shakuntalam operates as a mainstream commercial cinema screening popular feature films.

Inside, a long narrow foyer stretches the length of the single-rake, 365-seater auditorium. This has a small stage and curtained proscenium and is equipped for Cinemascope and stereo sound. When opened in 1972, all interior concrete surfaces were left exposed; later, acoustic panels were fitted on the walls of the auditorium and elsewhere the concrete was painted white. Long-term water penetration has resulted in severe damage to the concrete. In 2000 the cinema closed and the auditorium stripped for a complete refurbishment.

← *Three of Raj Rewel's massive exhibition halls are visible behind one of the open-air auditoria at the Complex.*

→ *The entrance of the Shakuntalam is on the left; the broad flight of stairs leads to the Falaknuma theatre on the roof of the cinema.*

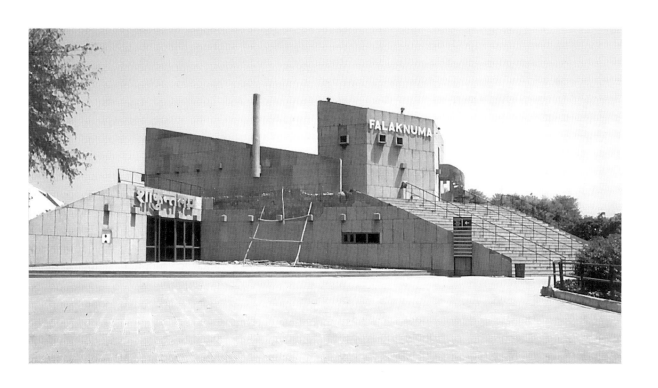

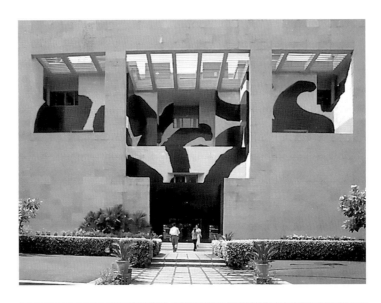

The British Council

Kasturba Gandhi Marg
New Delhi

The British Council Division of the British High Commission in India was inaugurated in 1950 and by the 1980s had outgrown its original premises. Funds were raised for a new building after it received a gift of a plot of land near Connaught Place from the Government of India.

Charles Corea (b.1930), India's most internationally successful, Post-Independence architect, started work on the designs for the building in 1989 and the new British Council building opened in 1992. His design is described as symbolising various elements of Indian history: the Hindu, the Mughal, the British Raj and the contemporary.[28]

Comprising two basement levels, three main storeys and a roof terrace, it houses a library, art gallery, meeting rooms, offices and a theatre. The building is faced in pink Rajasthan sandstone and the design incorporates a number of important works by British artists - a mural by Howard Hodgkin covers an inner wall and a sculpture by Stephen Cox is in the central courtyard. The entrance is approached through a formal railed garden from where an inner courtyard is visible through the glazed walls of the ground floor lobby.

Entered from this reception area, the multi-purpose theatre occupies one side of the ground and basement floors with dressing and green rooms on a lower level. The 206-seat auditorium is set on a steep rake, with boxes either side of the central projection booth on a slightly higher level. The walls are plain and clad with fabric, but in the deeply coffered ceiling, Correa introduces the unexpected: Classical Revivalism. The stage has no proscenium. When used for cinema shows, the screen is rolled down with black curtained masking.

Two 16mm Elmo projectors from Japan and a DDA stereo system are permanently installed and 35mm, DVD, laser disc and video are also available. Visiting companies bring in additional equipment for live shows. Films, both commercial features and documentaries, theatre, music and workshops are all part of an eclectic programming policy. Recent shows have included Steven Berkoff's *Shakespeare*, the rap artist Billy Business, Indian premieres of new British features films and the first demonstration in India by the IMAX Corporation of digital cinema presentation.

← *The main entrance to The British Council building. Part of Howard Hodgkins' mural is visible on the inner wall.*

← *The auditorium.*

Anupam-4

Sakat Community Centre
New Delhi

Anupam-4 is one of the first multiplex conversions in India. It opened in 1996 creating four new screens within the building previously housing the single-screen Anupam cinema. All four new cinemas are fitted within the old auditorium: Screen-1 a 368-seater, Screen-2 and Screen-3 both 150-seaters in the stalls area and Screen-4 a 332-seater in the old balcony. The cinema is in a wealthy, middle-class neighbourhood and although seat prices are high, it regularly achieves a full house. Computerised booking is available on its website.

A traditional cinema has been transformed into a Pop Art-style fantasy and the brash exterior gives only a hint of what lies within. Similar, vivid colours are employed inside, but enhanced by dramatic lighting effects. The main foyer floor for Screen 1 is laid in diagonal black and white marble bands from which a curved, chrome staircase ascends to Screens 2, 3 and 4 and a soda fountain. Gigantic faces of film stars - Monroe, Taylor, Garbo, Dean etc - in vibrant, Warhol-like screenprint colours decorate the stairwell. The refreshment area continues the theme and is decked out like a nightclub. The cinemas themselves are luxurious with very comfortable seating and high quality finishes but little decoration.

The striking thing about this building is that everything about it is quintessentially American. Outside the front entrance, this is epitomised by two rows of stars set into the pavement imprinted with the names of American film stars *à la* Hollywood Boulevard. A nearby Macdonalds and Pizza Hut completes the picture. The cinema is owned by an Indian entrepreneur in partnership with the PVR Corporation (Priya Village Roadshow), an Australian media conglomerate, which is planning to open similar venues in other Indian cities.

↑ *Anupam-4 – the exterior is painted in a brash blue and yellow colour scheme.*

↑↑ *A detail of the PVR website homepage.*

17. Shimla/Simla

Situated on a Himalayan ridge 2,200 metres above sea level, Simla was developed as a summer retreat by the British and became the official summer capital of British India following a visit in 1864 by the Viceroy. Every year, to avoid the heat the entire Government packed up from Calcutta and later Delhi and moved here transporting vast quantities of documents and belongings by horse and cart up to the hill station and then down again. In 1903, a narrow gauge railway opened from Kalka at the foot of the mountain made the journey up to Simla considerably less arduous.

The British called the place Simla; after Independence the name was changed to Shimla and it lost any national governmental role, but became the capital of the new State of Himachal Pradesh.

The buildings in Shimla, which cling to precipitous slopes along either side of the main ridge-top road, exhibit an extraordinarily eclectic mixture of styles: Gothic, Renaissance, Mock-Tudor, Arts and Crafts and even Swiss Alpine. After a visit in 1913, Lutyens is reported to have commented, "If one was told that it was built by monkeys all one could say was 'What wonderful monkeys!', but they must be shot if they tried to do it again..."[29]

Three cinemas – less than half the total before Independence – remain open all year for the present permanent population of approximately one hundred and thirty thousand, which is swelled by a large influx of holidaymakers during the summer months.

Gaiety Theatre
The Mall

When the British were in residence, the Gaiety Theatre was one of the focal points of the social life of Simla. Situated near the mid-point of The Mall, the main roadway running along the Ridge, the theatre is part of an 1887 extension to the Town Hall. After the somewhat dour, stone-faced Gothic exterior, the interior comes as a surprise: an exquisite Italianate opera house in miniature. The tiny horseshoe-shaped auditorium comprising stalls, surrounding boxes, dress circle and balcony is embellished with pilasters and moulded plasterwork decoration of gilded classical scrolls, foliage and flowers. The cast iron columns have gilded capitals bearing the Prince of Wales feathers. The recent restoration has brightened up the interior, but does not appear to be historically accurate.

An early visitor, the Vicereine Lady Dufferin, wrote of the Gaiety:

> It is a very pretty little place and is nicely decorated with pink muslin curtains in each box and gold and white paint. We sit near the stage and not only see the play very well, but all people in the theatre too, which adds to the amusement.[30]

The opening production was a comedy called *Time Will Tell* and since its inception, the theatre has been the home of the Shimla Amateur Dramatic Society producing seasons of straight plays and musical comedy. In the early years, touring artistes and occasionally small opera companies made appearances. Performances of Mascagni's *Cavalleria Rusticana* were given in 1901 and in 1908, both Paul Rubens' *Miss Hook of Holland* and Ivan Caryll's *The Toreador*. As most of the drama productions were wholly or partly amateur, those attending the Viceroy may well have been roped in; one show, for example, is reported to have engaged the services of Robert Baden-Powell and the script for another was written by a young aspiring journalist named Rudyard Kipling.

Despite the lack of permanent projection facilities, during the British Period the Gaiety served as one of the early venues commandeered by officials for showing 16mm prints of films brought out to India from Britain. This *ad hoc* role of presenting documentaries, educational films and newsreels continued up to Independence; since that time, film shows have ceased but the Dramatic Society continues in residence.

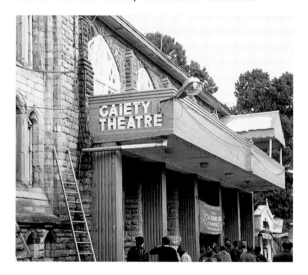

↑ *The Gothic exterior of the Gaiety Theatre. Part of the Town Hall extension is visible on the left.*

→ *The auditorium after the completion of the restoration work.*

Shahi

Lower Bazar

Entry to the Shahi is at roof level. The building clings precariously to the southern side of the Ridge and from above appears decidedly ramshackle. However, a far more attractive building with open verandahs accessible at stalls and balcony level is visible from further down the hillside. Originally operating as a drama theatre, it was converted into a cinema in 1932. From the roadway, patrons descend steep steps to the entrance lobby and a further flight of stairs to reach the 327-seater, two-level auditorium. Inside, the lobby and pay boxes have simple decoration, but elsewhere the cinema is completely plain. Seating is plastic throughout. In the projection box are two Cine Fine-Arc projectors c.1985 made in India and an unnamed mono sound system.

← *The Shahi from the bazaar – the entrance is at roof level.*

→ *The theatre verandahs seen from lower down the hillside.*

Rivoli
The Ridge

Perched on a ledge just below the ridge-top roadway, the Rivoli originally had a somewhat northern European appearance with a steeply pitched roof and overhanging eaves. The origins of the building are unknown, but it was converted into a cinema in 1935.

The small lobby, with classical decoration, was originally an open-fronted porch, but has had glazing fixed between the pillars. The pitch of the roof has also been altered. In the auditorium, all 348 seats are plastic, arranged as stalls, a shallow balcony and a row of six small boxes at the rear of the stalls with two or three seats in each. Apart from a few mouldings along the walls, balcony front and around the screen, the interior is purely functional. The projection box, approached by an external staircase and verandah above the main entrance, has two Peerless Magnarc projectors c.1940, an Ahuja Stereo system and an old unnamed mono amplifier. The cinema has no air conditioning; ventilation is provided by opening traps in the ceiling.

← *A view of Shimla on an old postcard - probably taken during the early years of the last century. The building later converted to the Rivoli is visible on the right hand side.*

↑ *The façade of the Rivoli. The stairs and walkway provide access to the projection cabin.*

18. Pune/Poona

Pune is 170 km inland of Mumbai, situated at an altitude of 560 metres and enjoying an equable climate. Once the capital of Maratha princes, its modern era began in 1817 when the British East India Company developed it as a hot season station for the Governor of Bombay; a cantonment was established which continues in use to this day. A residence was built for His Excellency and other lavish buildings, both public and private, followed.

The spelling was revised from Poona to Pune and nowadays it is a thriving industrial city and a major educational centre hosting one of the country's leading universities, the National Defence College, the Film & Television Institute and the National Film Archive of India. Some thirty cinemas serve a population of around three million.

Aryan Talkies

(Demolished)

Despite a popular outcry supported by the local press, the Municipal Authority demolished this historic cinema when its lease expired in 1983. It was built on land owned by the Council, but even after nearly twenty years the cleared site is still only a car park.

In Sanskrit, Aryan literally means noble and also refers to an ancient race that settled in Persia and Northern India. The Aryan, the first cinema in Poona, was opened in 1910 by Bapusaheb Pathak, who ran it until his death in 1970 at the age of 93 after which it continued under his son. As part of the campaign to save the cinema a video was made which included an interview with the son.31 Based on this, it is possible to piece together something of the appearance and history of the building.

Standing within a walled compound, the design was an extraordinarily eclectic, almost 'roguish' composition: mostly Gothic, but incorporating many classical and Mughal elements. The facade presented two gables with large Gothic windows separated by a portico comprising square classical pilasters and Mughal arches surmounted by an elaborate classical balustrade. Rearing above all was a tower of two stages, one with an open classical arch, the other with a spire topped by an enormous Gothic finial. The building may, of course, have originally served another purpose – possibly as a school or even a church.

During a period not identified, the cinema was the location of an unusual experiment apparently introduced to reduce eye strain. In the video is an old photograph of the auditorium showing sections of the seated audience facing in opposite directions. The commentary explains that an arrangement of prisms and mirrors allowed patrons in the more expensive seats facing one way to view a reversed mirror image, whilst the remainder in the cheaper seats facing the other way viewed the picture conventionally.

A typical programme at the Aryan commenced at 6.30pm, preceded by half an hour of music broadcast by loudspeakers in the compound. The one daily show would begin with slides, trailers and a newsreel, followed by a feature film. This format was common until the mid-1950s; thereafter more performances would be screened with extra shows of old films on Sunday mornings.

← *The exterior of Aryan Talkies and a portrait of Bapusaheb Pathak, inset (from a photostat of an unidentified newspaper picture)*

West End

Dr Ambed Kar Street

Now part of an unremarkable, 1980s multi-storey block, which includes offices and an hotel, this cinema replaces an earlier venue on the site that was demolished to make way for the new development.

The original West End opened in 1917 in what was then part of the cantonment area. A handsome building standing in a large, planted compound, it had a symmetrical, rendered facade, which displayed Mughal features in its three main entrance arches and *chajjas* below the roof parapet, but incorporated Art Deco styling in the fenestration. *(illustrated on page 24)* For many years, programmes included both films and stage shows with regular performances of traditional Indian dramas, musicals and dance entertainments. During the British era, Governors of Bombay, resident in Pune during the summer season, patronised the West End. Seats were reserved in the front row, but it is said the gubernatorial party would always purchase tickets. Despite such patronage and indeed what might be expected from the elegant exterior, the interior was mundane. The simple lobby had an internal pay box, but the auditorium was little more than four brick walls with a sheet metal roof. Arranged on two levels with 676 seats, it had a suspended ceiling of jute cloth and walls lined with jute blocks, but no decoration. At the time of closure, it was equipped for Cinemascope and to the last enjoyed a reputation as Pune's best picture house.

The old building was demolished in the early 1980s and its successor opened in November 1990. From the ground floor entrance, the stalls foyer is two storeys up. Lifts are available for the elderly and disabled, but most patrons must climb an exceptionally long and wide flight of stairs; the walls and treads of smooth dark stone are undeniably impressive but extraordinarily forbidding as an entrance to a place of entertainment. The foyers are equally austere. However, the sheer vastness of the spaces allocated for front of house facilities is exceptional. Seating in the auditorium, which accommodates 1,072 in cushioned tip-ups, is arranged in stalls and a sweeping cantilevered balcony. The Cinemascope screen has no proscenium or curtain, but its embrasures are painted mid-grey rather than the near-ubiquitous white. Downlighters and pendent air-conditioning outlets create diagonal patterns across the blue painted ceiling.

The West End is one of the three remaining houses in the Western India Cinemas Ltd. chain.

↑ *The new auditorium.*

Victory

General Thimaya Road
Cantonment

Located outside the city proper in the cantonment, this building originally served as a function hall for drama, musical evenings, weddings and dances under the name Capitol. When converted for cinema-use in 1945, the name was changed to Victory possibly in celebration of the end of the Second World War.

It stands in a large compound, enclosed by walls of linked arches and metal railings with spearhead standards. Probably dating from the late 19th century, the hall is built of brick with cement rendering and stone details, predominantly in classical style, but incorporating occasional Gothic embellishment. Seven round-headed entrance arches pierce the facade. A higher central section, crowned by a simple pediment is set forward of the auditorium hall. It has similar round-headed windows, which on the open verandahs either side alternate with carved Gothic quatrefoils. The roof is

tiled. Inside, the entrance lobby is impressive; a screen of round-headed arches on square stone piers with attached shafts and stiff-leaf capitals separates the small stalls foyer beyond. Three chandeliers hang from the ceiling and a fine stone staircase leads to the balcony level and verandahs above. The auditorium is purely functional and clad with acoustic tiles. A wide screen with plain embrasures was installed for Cinemascope in 1987 and although a curtain is present, it is no longer used. The cinema accommodates 630 on wooden seats in the stalls and padded in the balcony.

The projection box has Royal de-Luxe projectors from Japan with Westrex optics, old Westex sound equipment originally leased from Bush House, the BBC Overseas Service, in London and a recently installed Dolby system.

→ *The Victory is at the rear of a courtyard shaded by banyan trees.*

← *The lobby*

Prabhat
Appa Satara Road

After joining Baburao Painter's studio, Maharastra Film, in 1920, Rajaram Vankudre Shantaram (1901-1990), known as V. Shantaram, established his own Prabhat Studios at Kolhapur in 1929, moving to Pune in 1933. Shantaram had a distinguished career as actor, director and studio head. As a leading-man, he enjoyed a huge following especially among women, but his main claim to fame is as a director. Many of his social, mythological and historical dramas showed the influence of Germany's UFA Studios, which he visited in the 1930s. After leaving Prabhat Studios, he accepted the post of Head of the Government Film Advisory Board in 1941, but the appointment was short-lived as his strong Nationalist views were in conflict with the official Government line. He formed a new studio called Rajkamal Kalamandir in 1942 and twenty years later V. Shantaram Productions, both based at Parel, Bombay. Amongst his many achievements is the musical *Jhanak Jhanak Payal Baaje*, India's first Technicolor production released in 1955. His autobiography, *Shantarama*, was published in 1985.

Prabhat means Goddess of Dawn and the attractive logo employed by the studio is prominently displayed on the front of the building. Although the cinema was planned as a showcase for the studio's own output, the opening presentation on 21st September 1934 was Rouben Mamoulian's *Love Me Tonight* starring Maurice Chevalier and Jeanette MacDonald. During Shantaram's time, live drama and dancing shows alternated with film presentations.

Set at the rear of a railed courtyard, the rendered brick structure under a gabled roof was given a new concrete frontage during renovation works in 1974, but the original exterior with wooden balcony staircases is still partly visible. Formerly seating 722, this was increased to the present total of 894 all cushioned tip-ups arranged in a deep curve and with attractive metal standards. Little other decoration is present in the auditorium and acoustic cladding now obscures many surfaces, but vestigial stepped ceiling mouldings and Moderne streamline plasterwork are apparent together with concealed lighting which no longer works. The proscenium did not survive the renovation, being replaced by white embrasures, although the curtain is still in use.

The box is equipped with modified RCA Supreme-14 and RCA Photophone Imperial III projectors and a stereo sound system, all Indian-made. The cinema shows Marathi films for preference and some 'Bollywood' productions, which are much more popular.

↑ *A portrait of V. Shantaram is displayed in the foyer of the Plaza, Mumbai – another cinema owned by the Shantaram family.*

↑ The Prabhat façade after the 1974 modernisation. A version of the Studio's logo with a prominent sunrise is displayed in the centre of the façade.

→ A poster for Shantaram's 1955 film Jhanak Jhanak Payal Baaje – India's first Technicolor production.

→ The cover of the souvenir booklet issued in 1996 to celebrate Shantaram's Prabhat Studios depicting the studio's logo, the Goddess of Dawn sounding a horn in front of a stylised sunrise, above a picture of the studio buildings.

202   Pune/Poona

Liberty

Cantonment

In a large cantonment such as that at Pune, it was customary for the military authorities both before and after Independence to provide cinemas for service personnel. Run until recently by the Services themselves, many including this one have been sold off to private owners. The cinema opened in 1940, but the original name is not recorded and may have been something as prosaic as Defence or Camp Cinema. Its military role is possibly suggested by the V-shaped insignia of rank incorporated into the design of the surrounding compound walls. At one time, a small kiosk built into the front wall sold tickets when the cinema itself was closed.

Inside the gates is a dusty plot with a broken ornamental pool in front of the cinema hall. Behind the attractive, stepped facade with Art Deco window screens is a simple brick structure under a corrugated sheet roof. Access to the auditorium is through a small lobby.

← The façade of the Liberty.

The original cushioned seating having been removed, the cinema now only offers patrons fixed metal seats with wooden backs accommodating 526 on two levels. The interior is utilitarian and in a state of disrepair; seats are damaged, the concrete floor crumbling and holes in the suspended ceiling admit birds into the auditorium. A Cinelamp projector installed in 1982 and a 1985 Bakson are used with a Unisound mono system. An old Bauer Hi-tec valve amplifier is kept in reserve.

Situated in a somewhat remote military area far from shops and offices, attendance at the cinema is in decline. Despite being one of only two venues in the city presenting English-language films, average occupancy has dropped to about 25%. In an attempt to remain afloat, six shows of adult films are played daily to an exclusively male audience. A forlorn air hangs over the building as it awaits its probable demise.

National Film Archive of India

Law College Road

The trouble is we started sixty years too late and from the beginning we had to try to catch up at a time when nobody was even thinking about saving any old films. We were trying to collect, restore and preserve the heritage of Indian cinema before it all crumbled into dust.[32]

Whilst recalling the early days of the National Film Archive, its founding Curator and subsequent Director, B. K. Nair, offered two examples to illustrate the problems involved. Of the 1,300 silent films known to have been made in India, only nine survive complete, others in fragments and of India's first talking picture, *Alam Ara*, nothing exists but stills.

Much of the impetus to create a film archive came from Nair and his own extensive collection formed one of the core holdings of the new institution. Established in 1964 under the aegis of the Ministry of Information and Broadcasting, the Archive was originally housed within the nearby Film & Television Institute of India. This film school, in buildings of the defunct Prabhat Film Studios, trains directors, technicians and actors in commercial film production techniques.

Soon the Archive moved a short distance away to an old colonial-style bungalow, in fact a disused hostel for budding actresses. However, without its own auditorium, it had to continue to rely upon screening facilities at the Institute. With limited funds, it began the task of forming a representative collection of Indian film productions from the earliest days to the present and some important foreign films, together with a research library and viewing facilities. By the 1990s, the Archive had outgrown its bungalow home and a new building designed by a Government architect was constructed in part of the surrounding garden. It opened in 1994. The centrally placed auditorium forms the hub of the layout, which consists of two radiating arms, one housing the film restoration and storage facilities and the other the library and research areas. The Archive now holds over 12,000, mostly Indian, feature films and presents seasons combining film shows, lectures and debates mainly for students from the Film School and nearby University.

The auditorium is treated with reverence; as if entering a Temple patrons remove their shoes at the door and inside notices carry exhortations to refrain from chattering, eating or drinking. Seating 330 on a single rake, the design is somewhat reminiscent of London's National Film Theatre. The walls, with angled overhangs, are covered by a dark acoustic fabric between lighter coloured battens set in vertical patterns. It is air-conditioned, carpeted throughout and fitted with tip-up seats. The screen is in a simple, rectangular proscenium behind buff-coloured, velvet draw curtains and valance. Unusually, it is equipped with fully adjustable masking, enabling any film to be presented in the correct ratio. A second auditorium containing 20 armchairs, with a small curtained screen and facilities for DVD and video, is used for private screenings and seminars. A common projection room with a staff of two serves both auditoria, the main theatre using Tokiwa projectors and stereo sound from Japan, the small one Simplex IPC XLs from America.

← *The Archive's original bungalow home and the new headquarters.*

← *The main auditorium.*

Mangala
Shivajinagar

The Mangala is part of an exhibition chain in Pune and environs owned by the Chaphalkar Brothers, Prakash and Arvind. Their father, Appasaheb Chaphalkar, started the business in 1936 and today it is the leading film exhibitor in Western Maharashtra. This cinema, the last single-screen venue to be built in the city, was named after the owner's wife. It opened on 3rd July 1977 with Manmohan Desai's film *Chacha Bhatija*.

The building takes advantage of the steeply sloping site: entry doors in the front facade bring patrons into a lobby at balcony level. A canopy runs the full width of the cinema and returns along one side, where the entrance for the stalls is at a lower level near the basement car park. The name of the cinema is displayed high above the roofline of the auditorium at the top of a prominent fin. To one side of this feature is a relief of a dancing female figure, to the other are spaces for large attraction posters.

The architect Ramchandra Sadashiv Godbole was responsible for the layout and structure of the building; W. M. Namjoshi designed the applied exterior decoration and the entire interior decorative scheme. However, he was not given a free hand, the owners both strictly controlling his enthusiasm for ornamental excess and keeping a tight rein on expenditure. Nevertheless, despite or perhaps because of these constraints, Namjoshi produced one of his most restrained yet sophisticated interiors. The balcony foyer is the principal front of house area, a wide and pillared space with a marble floor, teak-cladding and mirror-panelled walls. Due in part to the low ceiling height, Namjoshi's elongated, glass waterfall chandeliers here appear somewhat stunted.

The auditorium tapers sharply towards the screen, which fills the entire wall without embrasures; the original scheme with a proscenium and curtain was not carried out. Bathed in soft amber light, huge plaster reliefs suggestive of unspooling film descend towards the screen along both side walls, trailing behind them is a thin black moulding representing a strip of celluloid silhouetted by flaring white light. For the ceiling, Namjoshi designed an acoustic membrane of reticulated fibrous plaster resembling solidified volcanic lava; overall, the effect is strange and organic. The 1,174 tip-up seats are on two levels and by extending the balcony back beyond the rear wall of the stalls, the amount of overhang is minimal.

The cinema is one of the few in India currently employing the latest projection technology. Equipped with both DTS and Dolby sound, it uses a platter system imported from Japan with Xenox optics. In addition are two Westrex Hi-Lite 35s.

→ *The exterior of the Mangala.*

→ Page 208 overleaf: *The auditorium with the dramatic feature of a spool and strip of flaring light along the side walls.*

City Pride
Satara Road

We are trying to sell a dream of entertainment to our patrons. The concept of a multiplex is new in India. Patrons expect a novel experience. They would come to a multiplex not only for watching movies but (also) for leisure and recreation. We would like them to experience the pleasure of fun-filled entertainment leaving all their personal problems behind. They should be able to focus on the entertainment hassle-free. The ambience and the experience we sell should make the patron come back for more and more and more and more.[33]

In these few sentences, Prakash Chaphalkar explains the concept behind the Chaphalkar Brothers new venture. City Pride is a four-screen multiplex which opened in 2001. The site on a busy main road was purchased in 1975 and the first scheme for a twin-screen venue was abandoned before any work started. Later, an hotel was constructed on part of the land but no cinema was built until work finally began in 1999 on the new multiscreen leisure complex. The largest auditorium has 1,235 seats on two levels, the other three, all single-floor auditoria seat 400, 250 and 50, the last a luxurious mini available for special shows and private hire.

The architect, Sudhir Ramchandra Godbole, is the son of R. S. Godbole, who some twenty years earlier designed the Mangala for the same firm. Uday Joshi, who has worked with Charles Correa, was responsible for the interior design. The building is raised on piers to provide the largest possible area underneath for parking - now regarded as a necessity for attracting a middle-class audience - and when tickets are purchased in advance, it will be possible to book a parking slot at the same time.

Moreover, to facilitate ticketing, purchasing points will be established around the city. Promotional schemes new to India, such as 'Happy Hour' and 'Prime Time' are planned as part of the marketing strategy.

The building is at the rear of the site; large open spaces to the front and side are for food vending and other attractions. The exterior is clad in gaily coloured stone with the name displayed on a large, centrally placed badge. Entry is directly into a vast, 12-metre high atrium, lit through one wall built entirely of glass blocks. On the floor are rows of pale blue stars set amidst dark grey marble slabs and the ceiling is a picturesque *trompe d'oeil* of sky and clouds. Electronic display panels and video screens provide up-to-the-minute details of seat availability and show trailers.

↑ *City Pride during construction in early 2001.*

↑↑ *Prakash Chaphalkar.*

The remainder of the ground floor is given over to other recreational activities: electronic gambling machines, children's facilities and refreshments as well as an art gallery and window-shopping displays. These are all open to the public, not just for those attending a film.

A feature is a pool and fountain beneath the glass-sided escalator that takes patrons to the cinema proper on the next level up. The foyer is designed to create the ambience of an upmarket disco with flashing multi-coloured lighting. One end forms a high level gallery across the atrium and wraps around the main auditorium as a large crescent-shaped space. The inner curve is taken up by a long refreshment bar between vomitories to Theatre-1. Entry to the two medium-sized theatres is opposite and on another level for the Mini.

Whilst using acoustic fabrics and boarding extensively, the overall effect in the four auditoria is far from austere. Great play is made with lighting effects. In the largest cinema, a flaring starburst arcs across the ceiling and tiny spotlights highlight diamond patterns on the walls. The screen is set inside a proscenium arch, which bears the owners' 'CB' logo at its centre. Less ornate schemes are employed in the other auditoria. All four are carpeted and a Pune firm that produces car seats for Mercedes Benz designed the sumptuous pushbacks, which besides being good ergonomically are easy to clean, repair or even replace between shows. Realising the potential for this product in India, the Chaphalkars established their own factory to manufacture them. Spaces are available for wheelchairs and this is one of the first cinemas in India where provision for disabled access has been considered at the design stage.

Projection facilities are divided between two cabins; one serves only the main auditorium, a floor below, another services the three smaller theatres. Equipment includes Kinoton projectors imported from Germany and Dolby, DTS and JBL sound systems. Computer controlled projection will enable the same film to be run with a fixed delay through more than one machine at the same time. It is envisaged that a sell-out presentation in one theatre could be shown with a short delay on a second or even third screen.

Unlike so many multiplexes in the West, the theatres here are not just functional boxes. Designed in a contemporary idiom using high quality materials and equipment, the City Pride re-creates something of the scale, magic and excitement of the old-style movie palaces and shows how attractive a multiplex can be.

← *The main foyer - in the centre is one of the vomitories to Cinema-1.*

→ *Page 212 overleaf: The lighting effects (from the top) for Cinema-1, Cinema-2 and Cinema-3 during the final stages of fitting out.*

19. Hyderabad

The State of Hyderabad was ruled by hereditary Nizams from 1724, who, despite the majority population being Hindu, were Islamic. At Independence, the Nizam resisted integration with the new India, but invasion by the Indian Army resulted in capitulation in 1948. Hyderabad is now the capital of the State of Andhra Pradesh and with a population approaching five million is one of India's largest conurbations and a major player in the computer and information technology industry.

The modern development of Hyderabad owes much to the seventh and last ruling Nizam, Mir Osman Ali Khan (1886-1967), who reigned between 1911 and 1948. Inheriting a near feudal state, he set about establishing modern organs of government, building irrigation schemes, founding hospitals and a university and endowing the city with many fine buildings. Gradually, the 19th century cantonment established nearby at Secunderabad merged with Hyderabad creating a contiguous 'twin-city'.

Film City, the production centre on the outskirts, is reputedly the most modern and best equipped in India, its facilities used by Hollywood and other international producers as well as indigenous filmmakers. Following a considerable number of closures in the last ten years or so, about seventy-five cinemas are still operating in the twin cities and environs.

Lighthouse
Abids
Old City

The Ruler of Hyderabad, His Exalted Highness Mir Osman Ali Khan, the 7th Nizam, was instrumental in the founding of this cinema. In 1922, with the Nizam's patronage, Dhirendraneth Gangopadhyaya (1893-1978), known as Dhiren Ganguly and a pioneer of film production in Calcutta, set up a new production company in Hyderabad called the Lotus Film Company. When the business expanded into film exhibition, this venue was one of two existing theatres in the Old City taken over and it was given the Company's name trading as the Lotus Cinema.

Born in Calcutta, Ganguly trained at Art College embarking on a career as a painter and photographer and in c.1915 he accepted a teaching post at the Nizam's Art College in Hyderabad. Upon returning to Calcutta in 1918, he formed the Indo-British Film Company with Nitish Chandra Lahari. This production company lasted some four years by which time Ganguly had established a reputation as a comic actor and director. After splitting with Lahari, he came back to Hyderabad at the Nizam's invitation to set up the Lotus Film Company, which produced several films and even established a film-processing laboratory in the city, but the venture was short-lived. A screening in 1924 at one of the company's cinemas of the Bombay-produced film *Razia Begum*, an historical romance involving a Muslim Queen and a Hindu slave, so displeased the Nizam that he promptly shut down the whole enterprise and banished Ganguly from the State. Moving first to Calcutta and thence to Bombay, Ganguly's film career continued on and off for another forty years.

When opened, the auditorium of the Lotus seated no more than forty, reserved exclusively for members of the nobility, the nawabs. With the change of name to Lighthouse in 1935, the seating was increased to 236.

The cinema is in a long classical terrace, the facade cement-rendered with pilasters and a parapet. Access to the auditorium is through an arched gateway, above which is a verandah with makeshift canopies, but whatever remains behind this facade is locked and barred. The cinema closed in the mid-1990s and will probably be demolished to make way for a shopping mall or apartment block.

↑ *Dhiren Ganguly in one of his comic film roles.*

← *The street frontage of the Lighthouse.*

State Talkies

Salar Jung Museum Road, Nayapool
New City

In the 1930s, Nawab Salar Jung Bahadur III was reputedly the richest man in Hyderabad after the Nizam. A collector on an indiscriminate but lavish scale, his City Palace has been described as ".... a curious mixture of the Wallace Collection and a junk shop..."[34] After his death in 1949, his daughters turned the Palace into the Salar Jung Museum.

Nearby is the Minar Garden Function Palace; dating from the early 1920s, this was formerly a cinema owned by the Salar Jung sisters. Originally called the Select and later Select Talkies, the name was again changed, possibly after Independence, to State Talkies. It operated a segregated audience policy: male and female patrons, including spouses, entered the cinema through different doors and were allocated separate areas of seating. Situated at the rear of a large garden enclosure secured by decorative metal railings and gates, the cinema is a steel-framed, cement-rendered building with brick infil. The front facade is symmetrical; a classical design with a recessed porch behind two carved stone columns, which rise the full height of the building. Fenestration and door details are Neo-Georgian. Along both flanking walls, open verandahs provide access to the two auditorium levels; at stalls level the doors are surmounted by large square decorative fanlights.

The cinema closed some ten years ago and the building now operates as a marriage and function hall. Front of house areas and the balcony have been closed off, but despite the insertion of a new lowered ceiling of fabric swags, the building itself has not been altered. The screen, projection equipment and seats have been removed and a new small stage constructed in front of the retained proscenium.

↑ *The exterior of the Minar Function Palace, formerly State Talkies.*

Yakut Mahal

Yakut Pura
Old City

Hyderabad's long-established diamond trade based in this area of the city is celebrated in the name of the cinema which means Diamond Palace. Built by Jaffar Nawaz Jung, his name in bold vertically placed letters once adorned the central stepped pediment of the facade. When opened in 1951 the building stood within a large, landscaped garden of lawns and flowerbeds set around a pool with a fountain illuminated by globe lights on fluted metal columns. Then regarded as the premier picture house in the Old City, its status has since deteriorated along with the surrounding area. The once elegant garden is reduced to a rubble-filled yard grazed by goats and chickens.

The cement-rendered brick structure is both fortress-like and in an Art Deco style with many of its decorative features picked out in primary colours. The original entrance, which is no longer used, opens directly into a marbled-floored foyer. Open verandahs behind moulded stone pillars along the flanking walls provide access to the auditorium stalls and a curved marble staircase leads to similar verandahs at balcony level. Nowadays, the pay box and entry is on one of the verandahs; the old foyer has been converted into a refreshment bar.

The two-level auditorium has 1,020 seats which are all original although many in very poor condition. Jutting out from the side walls, mid-way between the balcony and the screen, are two cantilevered boxes like a couple of minstrel galleries. Now no longer used, they contained special seats available only to married couples. Bald white embrasures surround the screen with no indication of a proscenium ever being present. Streamlined banding decorates the balcony front; otherwise, the walls are mostly plain and the ceiling has been clad with acoustic tiles.

For many years, the cinema ran first-run features; now, charging exceptionally low seat prices, it screens second-run Hindi films for a mainly young male audience. The original Peerless Magnarc/Simplex XL projectors together with a valve system Simplex XL mono amplifier are still in use.

← *The Yakut Mahal from the courtyard entrance.*

Shanti

Narayanguda Road
New City

Built in 1968-69 to the designs of an architect so far identified only by his family name Oke, the Shanti is a reinforced concrete building in a courtyard of palm trees. The sinuous curving shape of the exterior is clad in small pieces of granite set into a mortar rendering. Rising from ground level a wide hood-like canopy encloses the deeply recessed entrance. On either side, small randomly placed coloured rectangles and two vertical groupings of attenuated 'H' and 'U' shapes enliven the facade. The flanking and rear walls are faced with somewhat larger chunks of rough granite. Unusually for a cinema in India, the exterior of the building is completely free of advertising posters.

A row of glazed metal doors opens directly into the large, marble-clad foyer. Pillars subdivide the space which is decorated with figurative and abstract glass mosaic panels and illuminated by glass chandeliers. Only here are poster boxes advertising current and future attractions.

Curving around two circular pools with central fountains are spiral ramps leading to the balcony foyer and refreshment bar. Coloured, horizontal-banded panels cover the auditorium walls and finish at the rear of the stalls in a huge sweeping curve. The balcony front, dados and floor are of marble. Moulded convex and concave shapes with concealed lighting decorate the ceiling. Although without a proscenium, the huge screen boasts a fine, tasselled drop curtain. All 800 seats are deeply padded pushbacks; some in the circle are double 'family seats' with gold damask covers and reclining backs. The cinema screens Tegulu-language films and in the 1990s was upgraded to become a 70mm house with Venus projectors and DTS sound. A locally-based practice, Mahrendra Architects, began a programme of restoration in 2001.

↑ *The main entrance of the Shanti.*

Shanthi De Luxe

Himayatnagar
New City

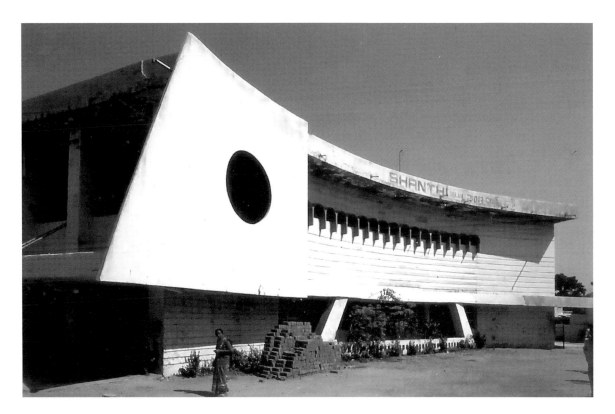

Opened as the Alaka in the mid-1970s, it received the new name Shanthi De Luxe following a change of ownership. The building is a dramatic asymmetrical structure of reinforced concrete, the curving upper façade supported on angled piers and the entire exterior painted gleaming white. Entry is through a long row of double glazed doors under a canopy created by the projecting upper storey. This leads to a large foyer and access to the plain auditorium accommodating 500 in a single rake. The cinema shows Tegulu-language films using old projectors from America and locally manufactured mono sound equipment.

Set back from the street, the only building on a very large plot in what is now an expensive part of the city, the Shanthi's future is uncertain: it may well be demolished and the site sold for redevelopment.

↑ The white façade of the Shanthi De Luxe.

Odeon 70mm
Odeon De Luxe
Mini-Odeon
RTC Crossroads
New City

Notwithstanding the use of the name, these cinemas apparently have no connection with the British circuit. In a large gated courtyard cum car park, two separate buildings house three Odeon cinemas, which in all employ a staff of over two hundred. The project began in 1987 with the Odeon 70mm, an 1,150-seat auditorium. Its architect was K. N. Srinivasan of Madras and Bangalore. Despite describing itself on both the canopy sign and in its advertising as "70mm," this cinema has only Cinemascope with Dolby sound. Its opening programme was Kashinadhuri Vishwanath's Telugu film *Srutilayalu* (1987). Ten years later in the second stage of the development, local architect M. D. Siddiqe created two extra screens in one new building: the 1,400 seat Odeon De Luxe and in the basement the 400 seat Mini-Odeon. This building is completely air-conditioned and includes a large underground car parking space. The De Luxe opened with another Telugu film *Iddaru* (1997) and the Mini with the American *Who Am I?*. The majority of the

presentations in the two big auditoria are Telugu-language features with other Indian language, foreign, or art house fare screened in the Mini-Odeon.

Both buildings are reinforced steel-frame structures with stone cladding and cement render colour-washed to look like stone. The interiors are cool and elegant with grey marble surfaces and exposed concrete beams. Both large cinemas have seating in stalls and balcony with some boxes on the upper level. The auditoria are rather plain with carpeting and luxurious seating but minimal decoration and the screens have no more than a hint of a proscenium, but use drop curtains. In the Mini, which is a single rake with one box at the rear, the plaster ceiling imitates a barrel vault and the walls are clad with teak.

The complex is enormously successful averaging more than 80% occupancy. Here it seems is an alternative to the usual multiplex: two substantial, traditionally planned cinemas and a smaller specialist house constructed as a group and run as one business sharing overheads and promotion expenses. A correspondent in *The Times of India*, under the headline "Cinema Halls' Rush" and calling Hyderabad "cinema crazy" describes the Odeon complex:

> .... at around 6pm.... the rush in these halls adds to the road-users' troubles. Even at 3pm, when most of the schools close for the day, the movie-goers too crowd the roads for the matinee show.... One way out of the problem could be to have broad pavements outside these halls and movie-goers should walk only on those.[35]

↑ *The first cinema - Odeon 70mm on the right; the later Odeon De Luxe and the Mini-Odeon occupy the building beyond.*

20. Jaipur

Jaipur, which translates as City of Victories, was formerly the capital of the Rajput Princely State. The city was founded in 1727 by Maharajah Sawai Jai Singh II (1688-1743) to replace the ancient capital at Amber 11kms distant. A ruler of great learning, especially in the sciences and mathematics, Jai Singh based the plan for the new city on a Hindu Vedic mandala, a pattern of religious and astrological significance comprising nine adjacent squares. At the centre of a formal layout of wide streets, a grid intersecting at right angles lined by elegant pink colour-washed terraces and arcades, is the City Palace occupying two of the nine sections in the plan.

Having outgrown what is now known as the Old City, a New City has since been built outside the old city walls encroaching into the surrounding desert. Although the palaces and havelis of the Old City overshadow later buildings, the New City boasts a number of Indo-Saracenic public institutions. Rudyard Kipling described Jaipur as "a pink city set on the border of a blue lake" and this description has remained attached to the city.

After Independence, Jaipur was made the capital of the State of Rajasthan and is a world-famous tourist attraction. Twenty cinemas operate in the city, which has a population of around two million.

Ramprakash
Chandi Ki Takshal

The Theatrical Institution was established in the year 1878 by His Highness the Honourable Maharajah Ram Singh Bahadur K.C.S.I., Imperial Councillor, C.I.E., for the entertainment and instruction of His Highness's subjects and for the civilisation of dramatic literature in Jaipur.

This notice on marble plaques in Hindi, Urdu and English in the entrance lobby describes the origin of the Ramprakash, a name derived from that of its regal benefactor in conjunction with prakash, meaning light. When it opened, the Ramprakash was regarded as the most modern theatre in India. Despite the absence of a fly tower and small backstage areas, it was able to produce dramatic stage effects such as props and performers rising from traps or appearing to fly in from the wings.

As befitted a reforming Ruler like Ram Singh II, the Ramprakash pioneered the then revolutionary idea of women performing female roles, but, because it was unheard of at the time for respectable women to appear on a public stage in India, the female parts were played by courtesans. Productions consisted principally of Sanskrit and Hindu dramas and these continued to be performed to great acclaim until the early 1940s, when, as a modernising gesture by the Government, the theatre was closed and converted into a cinema. It re-opened in 1944 with Jayantilal Deai's film *Tansen.*

← *Maharajah Ram Singh II (from an old postcard portrait)*

→ *The shuttered entrance of the Ramprakash with the painted scene of the Sun God, Surya, in the lunette. Above is a later Art Deco entablature bearing the name of the venue in Hindu script.*

After Independence ownership passed from the Royal Family to the new State Government of Rajasthan which leased it to private exhibitors. The cinema closed in 1988, since when it has been mothballed except for some dressing rooms and foyers used as storerooms by local shops and other peripheral areas as dwellings. The narrow theatre frontage is in the middle of a long, two-storey terrace of shops, with residential accommodation above, built in the traditional Jaipur style of stone dressings and pink colour wash on a cement rendering. Entry is through an archway flanked by classical columns under a moulded lunette containing a painted scene of the Sun God, Surya – the ruling Maharajahs of Jaipur claimed decent from the Sun. The façade is crowned by a later Art Deco-style, stepped superstructure, presumably installed when the building was converted to a cinema.

The theatre stands near the City Palace and is visible from its upper storeys. For the bulk of the structure housing the auditorium and stage areas, its unidentified architect ignored the local vernacular in favour of an Italianate classicism. Why this style was adopted is not known but from its external appearance this handsome building certainly would look more at home in a small Italian town than in the capital city of a Rajput desert kingdom.

Of brick construction under a pitched roof, the walls have a stucco finish with a golden-yellow colour wash. At the stage-end farthest from the street frontage, the building finishes in an apse with paired pilasters. The name of the theatre, facing towards the Palace, is cut in stone lettering on the cornice. Flanking round towers contain stone, spiral staircases, which lead to verandahs along both sides of the building to provide access to the upper level seating. The theatre is enclosed in a walled courtyard, nowadays covered with undergrowth and in front of the apse lies a broken pool and fountain

Members of the Royal Family attending the theatre entered from this end of the building. Women in purdah would be carried to one of the tower staircases in closed conveyances and proceed to special balcony sections screened by jalis on the verandahs and by purdah curtains inside.

When the cinema closed, the auditorium seated approximately 900 arranged as stalls and balcony, the later serpentine-fronted, supported on slender wooden pillars. Whatever slips or boxes originally existed along the sides were removed at the time the theatre was converted to a cinema, leaving most of the verandah doors below gilded lunette ventilators stranded half way up the wall. Above the main entrance to the stalls is a wooden carving of the Royal Arms of the former Princely State. The walls are plastered and painted pink with acoustic tiles only at the back of the hall. Pairs of hooks in the centre of the exposed timber boarded ceiling may once have held punkas. The screen, stage and dressing room areas are extant and in the projection box are two Peerless Magnarc projectors covered in dust sheets. The building is a protected monument and local talk suggests that it may be restored and re-opened as a cinema.

In the Audience Chamber of the City Palace is a model of the theatre in its heyday, appropriately displayed under a portrait of Maharajah Ram Singh.

→ *The view of the Ramprakash from the direction of the City Palace.*

226   Jaipur

Manprakash
Mirza Ismail Road

The Manprakash was the first cinema to be built in the New City. Although founded by the last ruling Maharajah of Jaipur, Man Singh II, Royal ownership ceased when it was sold to private exhibitors. The cinema was opened by the Maharajah on 2nd May 1935 and a newsreel film of the ceremony is shown in the cinema on each anniversary.

The architect and engineer Ramshya Mistry designed the building incorporating features reminiscent of the local vernacular style. The exterior is finished in a concrete rendering and the name appears high up atop one side wall. On the corner entrance canopies, Rajasthan architecture is depicted in the form of miniature fort walls. To one side of the building an outdoor waiting room has been created in a large walled garden of lawns, clipped hedges and stone benches.

The floor and walls in the stalls foyer are of inlaid marble. On the ceiling are Moderne box light fittings. Behind a stone screen of three Mughal arches a painted triptych depicts a Goddess flanked by peacocks, the latter being emblematic of the former ruling Maharajahs. At the top of the stairs to the balcony, which are enclosed by solid multi-coloured marble banisters, is a large Indo-Deco style roundel of the God Shiva. The balcony foyer has a jazzy green and yellow ceramic tiled floor and shallow Art Deco reliefs of classical inspiration cover the ceiling. Under multiple layers of advertising clutter, the original, streamlined refreshment kiosk has survived, apparently intact.

The 1,120-seater auditorium is arranged as stalls and balcony. Indirect lighting and rows of tiny spots highlight overlapping diamond-shaped panels on the ceiling and walls creating a tent-like canopy over the audience.

Lower wall areas are clad with corrugated wooden slats in geometric patterns installed to improve acoustics. Most surfaces are painted mauve or purple with cove edges picked out in red. When opened, this cinema had a marble-faced stage and a proscenium, now all removed. Arcolite projectors made by Cinesales Corporation of Delhi with their stereo sound system are used in the box and a mono Westrex valve system is kept as a backup.

← *The Manprakash - a miniature representation of traditional Rajasthan architecture decorates the corner entrance canopy.*

↓ *A portrait of Maharajah Man Singh II on display in the foyer.*

Polo Victory
Station Road

Two bothers, Kashva Ram and Kalanjee Shama, were polo stick makers for Maharajah Man Singh II of Jaipur whose team won the World Polo Championship in 1933. As a reward, the Maharajah, in truly regal style, gave the stick makers a plot of land on which to build a house. Nothing happened for more than ten years and then at the end of the Second World War, instead of building a house on the plot, one built an hotel and the other a cinema; hence the name of this venue.

The architect was Ramprakash Mohan Lal, who also designed the Stadium Cinema in Jodhpur. The foundation stone was laid on 14th December 1945 by the Maharajah and the cinema was opened on the 12th December 1947 by Earl Mountbatten, Governor-General of the Dominion of India. Both events are commemorated on marble plaques either side of the front entrance.

In an elevated position on a corner site, the cinema is approached up a broad flight of steps. A central, round tower with a wide quadrant canopy is flanked by two angled wings of offices. Stylised shields and spears recalling the State's martial past decorate the main entrance doors and on an exterior wall is a stone carving of a sun with a human face, a symbol of the former Princely State of Jaipur. *(illustrated on page 36)*

The entrance lobby is drum-shaped. Originally, a lightwell rose the full height of the tower, but in 1960

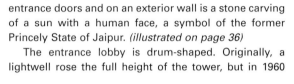

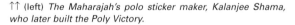

↑↑ (left) *The Maharajah's polo sticker maker, Kalanjee Shama, who later built the Poly Victory.*

↑↑ (right) *The Maharajah of Jaipur's polo team which triumphed in the 1933 World Championship, beating the British team by eight matches to nil.*

↑ *Eulab Chand's satirical painting of the victorious Jaipur team defeating the British in the 1933 Championship.*

← *Earl Mountbatten, Governor-General of India, cutting the ribbon at the Opening Ceremony.*

→ *The Poly Victory. The two commemorative marble plaques can be seen either side of the entrance doors.*

Jaipur   229

the top level was boarded over. Facing the main entrance is a large oil painting of 1946 depicting the polo match in which the Jaipur team captained by the Maharajah defeated the British. It is a satirical work based on a cartoon that appeared in *The Tatler* in 1933 showing the Jaipur team astride a charging elephant vanquishing their extremely foolish-looking British opponents, who are being scattered out of the way. At the time, of course, the painting also presented a potent political message. The artist was Eulab Chand, several of whose other works, including scenes of polo matches and portraits of the polo-playing Maharajahs of both Jaipur and Jodhpur, were formerly part of the cinema's decorative scheme. Persistent vandalism in recent years has forced the proprietor to remove these pictures for safekeeping and most front of house areas are now plain.

Still in place in the foyer lightwell are a sunburst feature and illuminated glass panels, decorative *jalis* in the form of stylised polo sticks cover stairwell window openings and the two boxy Art Deco-style sofas in the lobby look original.

The auditorium provides seating for 988 on three levels; the ground floor is arranged stadium style and confusingly called the Upper and Lower Circle separated by a wall running across the auditorium. The balcony is called the Noble Circle and above, either side of the projection booth, are two Royal Boxes, now disused but in the past reserved for the Royal Family and guests. Front stalls are fixed wooden seats with bench-like back supports, elsewhere are padded tip-ups. The small, rounded proscenium has a bow-fronted stage with a simple drop curtain, which replaced the original one of translucent silk and glass beads. Two huge, scroll-like

mouldings, which housed concealed lighting, sweep back from the proscenium along both side walls. The ceiling is obscured by acoustic tiles, but in an early photograph appears to have decorative mouldings.

In the projection box are two Bauer B12s imported from Germany in 1953 and recently installed Westrex stereo sound. An old Klangfilm mono system and the original slide projector and gramophone are still in place. The Polo Victory now screens only adult films.

↓ *One of the stairwell window jalis in the form of stylised polo sticks.*

Golcha

S. M. S. Highway

symmetrical and displays a number of Mughal details. Six paired pilasters rise two storeys to a *chajji*, above which is a large panel displaying the name of the cinema flanked by *chhatris*. Either side of the deeply recessed entrance doors inside the *porte-cochère* are Art Deco-style, wood and chrome-faced ticket offices. Before Independence, separate entrances were provided for the Royal Family and women patrons.

← *The inauguration of Premprakash Talkies in 1948 performed by the Maharani of Jaipur, Gayatri Devi, accompanied by the Maharajah, Man Singh II.*

↓ *The proscenium in the original 1948 auditorium.*

→ Page 232 overleaf: *The cinema exterior after the change of name to Golcha in 2001.*

→ Page 233 overleaf: *The completed Namjoshi lighting scheme in the auditorium.*

On 16th December 1948, the Maharani of Jaipur, Gayatri Devi, accompanied by the Maharajah, performed the opening ceremony of this cinema, which was then named Premprakash Talkies. Premprakash literally means Light of Love. The inaugural film was Ramesh Saigal's *Shaheed*. Later the name was shortened to Premprakash and in 2001, following the completion of major structural and decorative alterations, this was changed to that of the owners, who also run cinemas in Delhi and Bikaner.

Designed by the New Delhi architectural practice of Master, Sathe & Kothari Associates, much of their work has since been extensively altered, although the façade remains substantially as originally planned. Constructed of brick under a pink colour-washed, cement render, it is

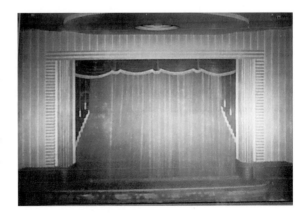

232   Jaipur

The auditorium was arranged on three levels: stalls with a raised section at the rear and above this a Royal Box fitted with purdah curtains, which could be closed when the house lights were up. A small square proscenium surrounded the screen furnished with valences and a green velvet curtain. A large circular light fitting decorated in a pronounced Art Deco manner dominated the ceiling and the walls were painted with stylised murals.

In 1980, the owner S. K. Golcha, grandson of the founder, planned a complete remodelling of the auditorium incorporating proposals for a lavish decorative scheme for the interior conceived by W. M. Namjoshi. A considerably higher and wider auditorium hall was constructed over the existing one. When complete, the old structure was demolished and a 70mm screen and huge rectangular proscenium was then installed. For many years, the auditorium remained in this state with the decoration on the walls and ceiling covered with boarding.

Eventually, some considerable time after Namjoshi's death, the lighting scheme was completed and his comprehensive design was revealed at last to patrons. Throughout the period of these works, the cinema remained open for business every day and building work was restricted to the hours outside show times.

At a grand inaugural ceremony performed by the Finance Minster of Rajasthan on 8th March 2001 with other Government Ministers in attendance, the cinema was renamed Golcha. The illuminated courtyard fountain in front of the building was restored for the occasion.

The foyers have been sympathetically modernised enhancing the original Art Deco design, but including only a few of Namjoshi's proposed changes. Here, the decoration is restrained, the new facilities luxurious and a sophisticated colour scheme of pale and deep blues is used throughout.

In the auditorium, however, the designer's distinctive extravagant style is given full rein. Namjoshi's recessed cartouches enclosing illuminated twining foliage and flowers are set in rows across the full extent of the ceiling and along both side walls. Within these recesses lighting effects can be varied from highlighting the décor in bright greens, pinks and reds to flooding the entire auditorium in an intense shade of blue, the colour of the carpeting, seat covers and velvet drop curtain.

The current configuration of 1,310 luxuriously padded seats are arranged in five classes: the stalls called Lower, Upper and Dress Circle, the mezzanine re-named Classique with the most expensive seats in the former Royal Box. This still enjoys its separate entrance from the main foyer. The projection box is equipped with two 70mm Super Cinex projectors and a Dolby sound system.

Notwithstanding the twenty years taken to complete this scheme, the owner is now planning to convert the auditorium into a triple-screen in such a way as to leave the new decoration unaffected.

↑ *The main entrance doors under the* porte-corchère *are flanked by streamline ticket offices. On the left is a section of the folding outer doors, which are decorated with silver reliefs on a turquoise background.*

Raj Mandir
Bhawandas Road

"Raj Mandir The Show Place of the Nation" proclaims a sign on the facade. There is certainly no false modesty here! Intended from the outset as a spectacular venue, the commission for the Raj Mandir was awarded to W. M. Namjoshi, who as both architect and interior decorator was given total responsibility for the design. With a considerable budget at his disposal, Namjoshi created an architectural extravaganza far more lavish than anything seen in his previous work. Moreover, for the first time he had the freedom to put into practice some of his ideas on cinema layout. One such concerned the foyer, which he believed played as significant a role as the auditorium in providing a setting for the all-important, communal experience of cinemagoing. Applying this theory at the Raj Mandir, Namjoshi adopted the simple or as his critics might say simplistic solution of dividing the available floor space equally between the two functions. The resulting vast foyer where all patrons could mingle before a show and in the interval as Namjoshi intended, did not prove popular with higher-priced ticket holders. In 2000 an additional foyer for their exclusive use was provided at balcony level.

'Raj Mandir' literally means the Temple or House of the King; but far from suggesting regal dignity, this cinema emphasises fantasy, indulgence and escapism. The playful exterior integrates the entrance canopy, cinema name and advertising poster in an asymmetrical design of zigzags, curves & stars. This declares unequivocally that here is a place of entertainment and pleasure. At night the facade is illuminated in gold and green, with the name of the cinema in orange standing out against the dark sky.

Entry is through teak doors pierced by turquoise glass in the shape of giant lotus leaves. A small, low-ceilinged lobby leads into the foyer, an enormous, double height, oval space in which every surface is richly embellished. Around the walls a continuous row of arches, both Mughal and Rococo in style and some with decorative fan vaulting, frame vases holding plant and fountain-like forms or cylindrical columns of light. A panel of backlit circles and sun shapes changes colour to form different patterns and shapes. Five huge cylindrical chandeliers are suspended from indirectly illuminated recesses. A long curving ramp with illuminated banisters of alternate inlaid teak and frosted glass sweeps up to the balcony level and restaurant. Before a performance the foyer is flooded in bright, warm-coloured light, highlighting the panoramic ornamentation; in the interval the lighting is dimmed and changes to cool greens and blues creating an ethereal, other-worldly effect.

Still more audacious is Namjoshi's scheme for the auditorium. Huge overlapping leaf forms and scrolls bathed in indirect light, extending across the ceiling and covering the walls, are carried up to the screen surround to form an undulating frame for the velvet drop curtain. The unprecedented scale of the decoration is thrilling. On entering before a show, the illumination is pale yellow and silver, then as the curtain starts to rise and in the interval these colours change to a deep glowing green.

↑ *The bust of the founder, Shree Ramjal Surana, in the foyer.*

→ Page 236 overleaf: *The auditorium lighting display:* (top)*, deep green - just as the curtain rises and in the interval, and* (bottom)*, silvery yellow – as the audience assembles before a show starts.*

→ Page 237 overleaf: *The exterior of the Raj Mandir at night.*

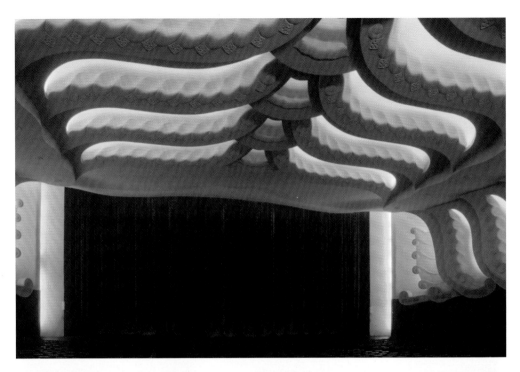

All 1,237 seats are luxuriously padded pushbacks arranged in four classes on two levels, the balcony being unexpectedly shallow. In the projection box are three 70mm Super Cinex projectors with Dolby sound.

The foundation stone was laid by the Chief Minister of Rajasthan and the opening ceremony on 1st June 1976 was performed by his successor followed by the first presentation, Ramanand Sagar's film *Charas*. A bust of the founder, Shree Rajmal Surana, who died shortly before the cinema opened, is displayed in the foyer. Ownership has now passed to his three sons.

Although the Raj Mandir has achieved nationwide fame and a reputation as one of the most remarkable cinemas in the country, it has not escaped criticism, both technical and aesthetic. Nonetheless, this cinema is important. Here, Namjoshi has reinvented the concept of the 'Dream Palace', where cinemagoers are beguiled by a milieu of opulence and fantasy which for most if not all is unobtainable in the real world outside. Many come just for the experience.

↓ *During the interval, the chandeliers glow silvery-blue amongst clusters of tiny twinkling lights in the ceiling and the illuminated banisters of the ramp stand out in the otherwise dimly lit foyer.*

Moti Mahal
Saudi Pai Singh Highway

The main structure of the Moti Mahal is boat-shaped with the curving side walls converging at both the front and rear of the building. A huge triangular window dominates the front façade, rising through two storeys from the entrance canopy to the roof. An adjacent tower, which accommodates a staircase, is enclosed at ground level by a single-storey office wing. Designed by the Jaipur-based architect Shaudhan Mal Dari, this is a steel-framed building with brick infil and clad in pink Rajasthan sandstone. It was opened on 9th May 1985 by the Chief Minister of Rajasthan.

The name Moti Mahal recalls Jaipur's jewellery trade; it means Pearl Palace and on the balcony foyer is an enormous, circular lighting fixture consisting of frosted glass pendants in the shape of oyster shells.

The auditorium, seating 1,245 in stalls and a balcony, tapers sharply towards the screen; hence the bow shape outside. Clumsy, blank arcades of round-topped arches decorate the side walls and a Plaster of Paris membrane with star-shaped interstices covers the ceiling. The floating screen with white embrasures has neither proscenium nor curtain. In the projection box, two 35mm Westrexs have been converted for 70mm and the sound system was upgraded to Dolby in 1999.

↑ The boat-shaped exterior of Moti Mahal.

Jawahar Kala Kendra
Jawaharlal Nehru Marg

To invent a new future and to rediscover the past is one gesture.

Carved on a standing stone, this quotation of Maharajah Jai Singh I faces visitors as they enter the Jawahar Kala Kendra. Dedicated to India's first Prime Minister, Jawaharlal Nehru, the J. K. K. is a Government-financed arts centre constructed on a green field site in the New City close to the University. It was designed by Charles Correa and built between 1986 and 1992. The President of India performed the opening ceremony on the 8th April 1993.

Inspired by the City of Jaipur itself, Correa adopted Jai Singh's formal layout of the planned city based on the Vedic Navgraha mandala comprising nine equal squares, each of which represents one of the planets both real and imaginary. In Correa's scheme for the J. K. K., nine units - either separate buildings or open spaces - are placed within a formal three by three grid. And as in Jai Singh's scheme for the city where one of the nine squares was displaced, so Correa, following this arrangement, sets one building in the complex at an angle – a shift of alignment used to create an entrance court. Designed as a series of individual but linked structures, the external walls are of red Agra sandstone and beige Dholpar stone dressings with the interiors painted off-white. Symbols of Jai Singh's nine planets are set into the dividing walls. Entry to the main offices is under a domical space decorated by a Jain cosmograph depicting an earthly manifest: land, rivers, mountains, animals, vegetation etc.

The facilities of the Jawahar Kala Kendra are open to all: a library, galleries and classrooms surround a large outdoor theatre-in-the-round seating 1,500 that occupies the central of the nine squares as a symbolic empty space. The one building set at an angle, representing Shakra or the planet Venus, houses two auditoria. Designed as a reinterpretation of a Rajput fort, a warrior and his wife stand guard on plinths either side of the entrance. Inside is another but much smaller, theatre-in-the-round and a multi-media venue with a proscenium and seating for 230 in a steeply raked stadium layout. This second auditorium is fully equipped as a cinema with a retractable screen. Plain walls contrast with an exposed concrete, egg-crate ceiling. Small backstage areas and dressing rooms are provided, but no fly tower. The projection box is equipped for 35mm, 16mm and slide projection with a stereo sound system.

Initially film shows were a regular attraction; recently these have been reduced to alternate weekends with dramatic and musical performances now occupying most of the programme schedules. More use is made of the cinema facilities, however, in conjunction with other activities at the Centre such as seminars, exhibitions or performances in the main open-air theatre, when feature films, documentaries and art films linked to these activities are presented.

← *The auditorium building, the one structure in the Jawahar Kala Kendra set at an angle to the main axis of the complex - a feature echoed in the surrounding paving of the entrance court. In the mandala adopted by Correa, the star above the auditorium entrance represents Venus.*

Alka

Vishavkara Road

The Alka is a cinema in the making. Unfinished, with bare concrete walls and floors awaiting decorative surfaces, the first auditorium called Alka-1 opened on 27th March 2000. The 945-seater arranged on two levels is equipped with two 35mm Cinemascope projectors with Westrex 14 light sources and a DTS sound system.

Every day after the last show, construction work proceeds through the night on a second auditorium, Alka-2, being built above Alka-1. This will be a single floor of c.300 seats with separate projection facilities. The foyers are already complete; all walls and floors are marble throughout and eventually both auditoria and the exterior will be faced with decorative cladding. The architect, Vijay Gupta of New Delhi, previously designed the Ankur cinema also in Jaipur for the same client.

Planned as a venue to serve a local community, the Alka complex is situated in a new, working-class suburb on the outskirts of the city. It proposes to programme mainstream box office hits in Alka-1, less popular films or re-runs in Alka-2 and if warranted run a single print of a blockbuster in both cinemas concurrently with staggered start times.

↑ *The architect's perspective of the proposed exterior of the Alka.*

21. Jodhpur

The erstwhile capital of the State of Marwar - literally Land of Death - Jodhpur was founded in 1459 by the Raiput Prince Rao Jodha and is a dramatic walled city with the Meherangarh Fort towering some 130 metres above the surrounding blue colour-washed houses.

In addition to the Fort, Jodhpur possesses other architectural set pieces in the new city built outside the old walls: late 19th and early 20th-century buildings in Indo-Saracenic style by Sir Swinton Jacob and since Independence, the University complex by Uttam Jain. Most notable, however, is the vast Chittar Palace designed by Henry Vaughan Lanchester with its own cinema theatre.

Jodhpur is now part of the State of Rajasthan and second in size to Jaipur. Currently its population of approximately one million is provided with ten cinemas, not one of which pre-dates Independence.

Ali Akbar
Umaid Bhawan Palace

Approached at twilight, the vast, flood-lit Palace set on a hill against the Jodhpur night sky resembles nothing less than a fabled stronghold out of the Arabian Nights. In fact, it is one of the most remarkable 20th-century buildings in India. Built between 1929 and 1944, it was part of a massive programme of works instituted by the Ruler, Maharajah Umaid Singh (1902-1947), and designed to alleviate poverty among his subjects by providing employment. The opening ceremony took place on 14th February 1943, when the Maharajah's eldest son turned a key to unlock the great front door.

The architect was Henry Vaughan Lanchester (1863-1953). He was responsible for a considerable amount of work in India including an hotel in Calcutta, the Post Office at Lucknow and town planning schemes for both Delhi and Madras, but his reputation rests primarily on a number of major British public buildings in the grand Neo-Baroque manner such as the City Hall and Law Courts at Cardiff (1897, with James Stewart and Edwin Alfred Rickards) and the Wesleyan Central Convocation Hall, Westminster (1905, solely with Rickards). In partnership first with Geoffrey Lucas and later T. A. Lodge, he formed what eventually became Lanchester, Lucas & Lodge. Lanchester was one of the founders of the Town Planning Institute, for two years editor of *The Builder* and later, Professor of Architecture at University College, London.

Situated on Chittar Hill on the outskirts of the City of Jodhpur, the Palace is frequently described as an amalgam of Indo-Saracenic, Classical Revival and western Art Deco. However, an alternative interpretation[36] suggests that the Maharajah and his architect looked to Buddhist and Hindu antecedents in the Temple Mountain-Palaces of Burma and Cambodia and in particular to Angkor Wat. Lanchester is known to have researched these structures and their layout, construction techniques and refined use of imagery are likely precedents for the Jodhpur Palace. Moreover, all over the building are examples of sculpture depicting traditional Hindu symbols mixed with those of the Rajput Royal Family. Comparable with much Art Deco sculpture of the period, this work was supervised by the sculptor J. Roslin and executed by local craftsmen. For the interior, the Polish artist Julius Stefan Norblin produced murals complementary with the Art Deco furnishings he designed after the original furniture ordered from Maples in London was lost at sea en route to India.

As a descendant of warrior Rajput Princes in an age when martial exploits were forbidden, Umaid Singh directed his energies into modernising the State government and welfare organisations. He was fascinated by the new technologies being, for example, a keen aviator and motorist and like most Maharajahs of his time had a large collection of motor cars. One wonders if he possessed a Lanchester! The Maharajah embraced the new medium of moving pictures and a theatre cum cinema was part of the original design of the Palace.

At the end of one of the seemingly endless, ground-floor corridors, a small sign above a door announces the name of the theatre, Ali Akbar. The auditorium is impressive, constructed entirely in pink and white sandstone; the transverse arched ceiling consists of moulded panels pierced by decorative air vents. A small, curved stage is surrounded by a high, arched proscenium. Steeply raked stalls accommodate an audience of 120 on cushioned, rexine-covered seats with black wooden backs.

↑ *A portrait of Maharajah Umaid Singh in the Palace.*

← *The floodlit Chittar Palace, now Umaid Bhavan Hotel. (a detail from an hotel display) The cinema is located in the projecting wing below the foreground square tower on the right.*

On a raised platform at the back of the auditorium behind a row of pillars and screened by low metal railings is the Royal Box with six low chairs in richly embroidered covers. This higher level extends along either side behind pillars and low screens creating a narrow passageway to doors leading to the private apartments.

Following the Government's final removal of regal privileges in the 1970s, the then Maharajah, Gaj Singh, transferred the property to a Trust and in 1977 it opened as the Umaid Bhawan Palace Hotel. Every evening from October to February English-language films are screened in the cinema for the entertainment of hotel guests. The stage has lost its curtain and the present screen is a somewhat makeshift affair. All original equipment has been removed and it now employs a laser disc system with Dolby sound.

↓ The auditorium looking towards the Royal Box behind the row of stone columns at the rear of the stalls.

Stadium
Stadium Road

↑ *The exterior of the long-closed Stadium – on the roof, the carcass of its neon sign is still in place.*

↑↑ *The two shrouded Photophones in the undisturbed projection box.*

The naming of this cinema is explained by its proximity to the city's public athletics stadium; both were built by Maharajah Umaid Singh for the use of his subjects. The cinema is by the same architect as the Polo Victory in Jaipur, Ramprakash Mohan Lal, and dates from the late 1930s or early 1940s.

The understated, streamline-style of the exterior is slightly reminiscent of some small town cinemas built in England at the time. A symmetrical frontage with rounded corners has a broad flight of steps up to the entrance under a thin canopy. The metal skeleton of a former neon sign stands on the roof. Just inside the entrance, a large, colourful mural depicting a Hindu mythological scene decorates one of the lobby walls.

The two-level auditorium had a capacity of 850 with two large boxes at the back of the balcony; one formerly reserved for the Royal Family. The front and rear stalls are separated by a wall running right across the auditorium, obliging patrons with front stalls tickets to use a separate side entrance and for comparable reasons, decorative metal stairway gates bar the route from stalls to balcony.

The cinema closed over twenty years ago. The exterior is in good condition, but inside, everywhere is thick with dust. Guarded by a punctilious caretaker, the projection box still houses two Photophones slumbering under shroud-like covers as if awaiting the call to flicker back into life.

Kalpataru

Sector E, Sindhi Colony

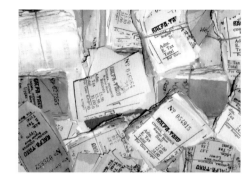

Mumbai-based Uttam Chand Jain (b.1934) is one of a number of architects practising in Post-Independence India, who, whilst accepting the precepts of Modernism, seeks to marry these ideas with traditional Indian architectural forms. In a number of projects in the State of Rajasthan, Jain has employed elements of both the style and where possible the techniques of the local vernacular. The resulting buildings, functional and modern as they are, bear the hallmarks of the traditional desert architecture of the region. Between 1970 and 1985, he designed several buildings for the University of Jodhpur, steel-framed structures but at the same time employing traditional masonry techniques.

The Kalpataru opened on 4th April 1982. Externally, the building is severe and relates closely to Jain's University buildings in the city, whereas the interior is far more light-hearted. The sheer exterior walls are constructed of local golden-coloured sandstone in lime mortar jointing and topped by a wide parapet with the cinema's name in large letters. The entrance is set deep within a huge, rectangular portal with the name of the cinema on a brightly coloured mosaic panel in Hindu script.

Foyer floors and stairs are of pink Rajasthan marble and a speckled plaster composition imported from Japan has been used to coat the walls. In the balcony foyer, bold zigzags and rows of arrowheads decorate the walls; the ceiling is divided into angular sections by mounted triangular strips painted bright yellow. On the walls in the auditorium are bold diagonal stripes and abstract block patterns in panels. The screen is without proscenium or curtain. The cinema accommodates 1,054 on two levels; the front stalls are crude wooden seats

and patrons are provided with lidded spittoons along the side walls. Rear stalls are padded tip-ups. The balcony is furnished with cushioned pushbacks with a headrest, their metal standards displaying a large embossed 'S' trademark. In the projection box, two Westrex Hi-Lite 130s have been in use since the opening. Dolby sound came later.

↑ *Bundles of used ticket stubs – the exhibitor's basic admission charge is doubled by the 100% Entertainment Tax levied in the State of Rajasthan.*

→ *The monumental exterior of the Kalpataru.*

↓ *Cushioned pushbacks with headrest in the balcony.*

Gehir Mandir

Nai Sarak, Old City

The Gehir Mandir opened in 1987 and with a seating capacity of 1,473 is one of the largest cinemas in the State. It is owned by the Moliani family, whose members have been involved in cinema exhibition for three generations. The site for the cinema was carved out of solid rock; the sloping ground was excavated to enable the cinema to be set back against a vertical rock face. The lively exterior mixes pink and yellow stone in wide horizontal bands with a large mural covering most of the façade above the canopy depicting Krishna, Radha and other Hindu Gods.

The Hindu theme continues in the highly decorated interior, which is finished in marbles, brass and painted moulded plaster reliefs. Along one side of the stalls foyer, niches between tiered uplighters display plaster reliefs of Hindu Deities. At the far end, a fountain plays before a garlanded bust of Purumal N. Moliani, the founder of the cinema and father of the present owner. Mirrored strips containing rows of tiny flashing bulbs

illuminate the ceiling interspersed by concentric recessed bands housing indirect lighting.

In the balcony foyer, the soffit of the rear balcony ramp forms a steeply sloping ceiling. During the daytime, dramatic effects are created by sunlight streaming in from a continuous row of tiny windows at the top of the external wall; at night, the exposed concrete ceiling is illuminated by thousands of tiny light bulbs. Along one wall, a series of elaborate, bronze-finished plaster panels illustrate The Ages of Man from birth to death in Hindu mythology.

Decorating the auditorium walls and ceiling are brightly-coloured reliefs showing Hindu scenes within swirling moulded cartouches. Elsewhere, the surfaces are covered with perforated Plaster of Paris acoustic panels. The screen has no proscenium or curtain and is surrounded by white embrasures. Seating is all padded pushbacks except for the unusual feature of 3-seater benches at the back of the balcony.

The projection booth is fitted with two Westrex Hi-Lite 130s made in India and an unnamed stereo sound system.

↑ The final panel of the sequence illustrating The Ages of Man in the balcony foyer.

← The Gehir Mandir – the sheer rock wall at the rear of the cinema is visible on the right.

22. Bikaner

Founded in 1488 as an independent kingdom by Rao Bhika, a son of the founder of Jodhpur, until Independence Bikaner was the capital of a Princely State ruled by Rajput Maharajahs. Although a remote desert kingdom, its prosperity in earlier times was due to its propitious situation on trade routes to India's ports, in particular, the famous Silk Route.

In the city, the mediaeval Junagarh Fort embracing a number of opulent palaces is one of India's most notable monuments of the Age of Princes. In addition, the 20th-century Lallgarh Palace, built on the outskirts for the last reigning Maharajah, Ganga Singh, is an outstanding Indo-Saracenic structure, generally considered Sir Swinton Jacob's masterpiece.

Noted for camel breeding and the famous Camel Corps, which saw action in the Second World War, Bikaner, now part of the State of Rajasthan, is in one of the poorest regions of the country. The City with a population of about seven hundred and fifty throusand has only five cinemas.

Ganga Theatre

Ganga Niwas Public Park
The Collectorate

The penultimate Ruler of the State of Bikaner, Maharajah General His Highness Sir Ganga Singh Bahadur (1880-1943), was a remarkable man. He modernised the Government, built the Ganga Canal, bringing much needed irrigation to his desert state, and was a highly regarded Empire statesman in the days of the British Raj, representing India at the Peace Conference of 1919. Notwithstanding these significant achievements, Ganga Singh's ultimate historical importance may well rest more upon his abiding obsession with photography. Not, however, for his own photographs if he ever actually took any himself, but rather for employing a large staff of photographers to record every detail of his life and reign. The resulting archive of well over 30,000 images depicting regal life at the end of the British period is held at the Museum he established in the Lallgarh Palace.

Another of the Maharajah's great enthusiasms was the cinema. In the Museum, an early silent projector modified for sound testifies to private screenings in the Palace. Later in the 1930s, he built a public cinema in the city as an official State project. A Committee appointed to undertake this task recorded in official files[37] the detailed administration of the construction without, regrettably, once mentioning the name of the architect. It is possible a member of the Committee, the Chief Engineer a Mr Mackenzie, may have so acted. After the building was completed in 1935 it was leased to a private exhibitor, Seth Shri Gopal Mohta. Following Independence, ownership passed to the Rajasthan State Government which leased it to the Golcha Group and it continues under that management.

Named in honour of its founder, the building was designed for both live drama and film presentation. According to the official file, it was built "...in a traditional Rajputana style" of sandstone with pink colour wash render under a pitched roof. Large, square-set and imposing, the facade displays a mixture of Indian and European details: the entrance canopy and zenana porches are supported by classical columns, but above a *chajja* the parapet is in the form of Mughal battlements.

Like most of the interior, the large rectangular lobby has an exceptionally high ceiling and is somewhat reminiscent of a booking hall in a Victorian railway

← *Portrait of Maharajah Sir Ganga Singh Bahadur in the Lallgarh Palace.*

→ *The Ganga Theatre - just visible is the Mughal pediment on the rear of the auditorium.*

station. On one side an original but long-disused ticket office with delicate, carved wooden filigree survives. Unexpectedly, the balcony foyer is furnished with a European style fireplace, installed no doubt to warm royal and noble patrons during cold desert nights. Still hanging from the ceiling are the remains of a damaged wooden chandelier, a reminder of grander days. Wide and lofty corridors and a sub-basement ambulatory surrounding the auditorium provide welcome air circulation helping to keep the interior cool in the scorching summer heat.

When opened, the theatre had an orchestra pit, a deeply moulded, rectangular proscenium of classical design with dressing rooms and a green room backstage. Installation of a wide screen in 2000, however, resulted in the removal of the proscenium and its curtain, but the stage and orchestra pit were left. The auditorium consists of stalls and a balcony with five boxes at the rear, seating 906 in all. The 1940 Theatre Plan shows the balcony divided into three boxes: two zenana boxes and one reserved exclusively for the Royal Family, all out of

↑ *The Ganga auditorium after the removal of the proscenium.*

← *The balcony foyer with its European-style fireplace and remains of a chandelier.*

Ganga, in effect a Command Performance. When the Viceroy, Lord Linlithgow, visited Bikaner in 1937 as part of the Maharajah's Golden Jubilee celebrations, he was His Highness's guest of honour at a special performance of the Tom Walls' film of Ben Travers' *Foreign Affaires* (1935) supported by a Walt Disney cartoon - an ironic reminder of the might of Empire assembled in State to watch Mickey Mouse and a Whitehall farce!

← *The original ticket office with teak panels of finely carved vines and flowers.*

↓ *The Souvenir Programme for the Mahrajah's Golden Jubilee presentation at the Ganga Theatre.*

bounds to the public until the coming of democracy and the disappearance of purdah. Some original decoration is preserved: on the walls and balcony front is a continuous frieze of blind Mughal arches and a chandelier is suspended from the otherwise unadorned ceiling.

Access to the projection box is by vertical ladder. Equipment comprises two RCA projectors adapted for Cinemascope brought from the Delhi Golcha in the 1980s and a Cinécita-100 Solid State amplifier from the Premprakash in Jaipur, now superseded by Dolby sound.

During the Maharajah's reign, the Ganga acted as a virtual 'Cinema of State'. Material on file records the Maharajah's frequent demands to see particular films. One such, a Bombay newspaper clipping advertising Vivien Leigh in Alexander Korda's *Lady Hamilton* (1941), was sent to the cinema manager bearing the Royal hand-written request for a screening as soon as possible at the

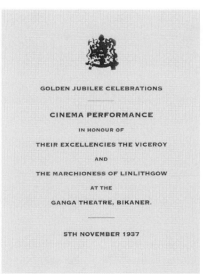

GOLDEN JUBILEE CELEBRATIONS

CINEMA PERFORMANCE

IN HONOUR OF

THEIR EXCELLENCIES THE VICEROY

AND

THE MARCHIONESS OF LINLITHGOW

AT THE

GANGA THEATRE, BIKANER.

5TH NOVEMBER 1937

23. Mysore

Mysore, once the capital of the former Princely State, is now the second largest city in the State of Karnataka with a population approaching eight hundred thousand. Situated on a plain some 800 metres above sea-level, the city has been described as the most beautiful in India; a place of parks and palaces gently scented with incense and sandalwood, its principal products.

A relatively small-scale (in Indian terms) film industry, together with that in the nearby city of Bangalore, specialises in Kannada (the local language) and Tamil-language films. However for their programmes, Mysore's twenty-five or so cinemas draw primarily upon product from Chennai and 'Bollywood'.

Sheekrishna

City Circle

That the Sheekrishna was once a building of some importance is demonstrated by the imposing exterior and prominent location at the principal road intersection in the city centre, yet it has been abandoned for nearly half a century. Opened as a drama theatre in c.1897 and converted to a cinema sometime before Independence, it has been boarded up since closing in the mid-1950s, half-hidden behind a circumjacent parade of ugly lockup shops.

The richly ornate facade incorporates Indian and Western details, mixing classical pilasters, balustrades and fluted columns with *chhatri*-like structures at the corners. Many of the Georgian-style windows have fanlights, some still with shattered fragments of coloured glass. Finely carved, wooden columns supporting a verandah along one side of the auditorium may have been rescued from the ruins of the City Palace, which was destroyed by fire at about the same time this building was under construction.

The theatre was built over accommodation for shops

and other businesses that occupied most of the ground floor. In the small entrance lobby, a grand, carved stone staircase leads to a narrow gallery with access to the first floor auditorium, a plain single floor raised in a series of wide, shallow steps. The exposed, boarded roof and sections of decorative metal railings are intact; otherwise, the interior has been stripped and of the projection box nothing is left but the portholes. Despite its current state of disrepair, the building may be saved: plans are in hand to restore it for use as a marriage hall.

↑ *The external booking office window surrounded by the remains of old film posters.*

↑↑ *A detail of one of the finely carved columns that may have been rescued from the City Palace after the devastating fire.*

← *Part of the theatre façade visible above the surrounding shops.*

Woodlands
Church Road

With a little stretch of the imagination, Woodlands would not look out of place in somewhere like Tunbridge Wells. Built as the General Post Office in the late 19th century, it was converted to a theatre after the Post Office moved out. This operated as a live venue for a few years prior to becoming a cinema around 1922.

The classical façade, lobby and staircase date from Post Office days. Most of the remainder of the building was gutted for the conversion and as a consequence of squeezing a theatre on a diagonal axis into the lozenge-shaped site the auditorium widens rather than narrows towards the screen. Seating for 765 is arranged in stalls and balcony. Decoration amounts to a few mouldings on parts of the original building along the side walls, but in 1969 the ceiling and most other areas were obscured by acoustic tiles. The screen is without a proscenium or curtain and nothing has survived back stage.

Two walls of the projection box, a survival of the original building, jut out at forty-five degrees into the auditorium and the two Photophone Superarcs project through portholes angled like squints. Sound is provided by a TCX-Smart Stereo system.

↓ The large number of motorcycles parked outside the cinema is an indication of a good house for the matinee show.

Opera DeLuxe

Albert Victor Road

The Opera DeLuxe opened in 1921 as a theatre with full backstage facilities for live drama and possibly opera and musical entertainments as well. Not long after, it was converted to a cinema and with the advent of sound and a new owner, the name changed to New Opera Talkies. Following extensive remodelling in 1950, which included a new façade, the cinema reverted to its former name. However, both names remain on the façade and in the lobby. Two additional small rooftop name signs are in working neon. A blank, stepped superstructure above the original entrance may once have displayed the name or an attraction poster.

The building is of brick with a later cement render. A first-floor verandah connects two drum-shaped, corner entrance towers: one is used as the lobby, the other, together with back stage areas blocked off during a subsequent refurbishment in 1984, is now occupied by an auto repair workshop. At the same time, projection equipment was upgraded to two Photophone Superarcs but the Photophone Futura mono sound system was kept in service.

Art Deco mouldings and grilles survive in the circular lobby. The 989-seat auditorium has retained its theatrical layout, arranged as stalls and a balcony with slips although these no longer have any seats. Most of the decoration has disappeared, either removed or obscured under acoustic cladding, yet despite the removal of the proscenium the drop curtain remains in use.

→ *Opera DeLuxe at dusk. The entablature above the original entrance is on the left.*

Lido

Church Road

On the death of the firm's founder, Laxman Mahadedeo Chitale, his son Srikrishna Laxman Chitale succeeded as principal architect of the Chennai-based practice L. M. Chitale & Son. Notwithstanding his father's outspoken advocacy for the continuation of an indigenous architecture employing traditional building crafts, under his son's influence the firm repudiated Indian styles, turning instead to sinuous modernist forms: the Lido is one such building.

Land owned by the Roman Catholic Diocese of Mysore was leased specifically for the construction of a cinema and the Bishop laid the foundation stone of the Lido on 20th February 1972. Considered the premier venue in Mysore, it shows only first-run films in the original language, Hindi, Tamil or English.

The central, front section of the upper storey is a continuous, serpentine wall of glass. Elsewhere, exposed concrete surfaces have an irregular textured finish and along one side an oversailing upper storey provides shade for the exterior ticket office and waiting area. A long row of glazed doors allows entry to the vast, sparsely furnished front of house spaces. Here, bold primary colours highlight plain areas of terrazzo, marble and exposed concrete. A cantilevered staircase of brightly painted steel connects the three foyer levels and a refreshment bar. In the attractive but plain auditorium, 856 seats are arranged in stalls, circle and small balcony. The projection box uses two 70mm Photophone Widearcs and since 1999, Dolby sound.

↑ *The exterior of the Lido.*

24. Chandigarh

Partition in 1947 placed Lahore, until then capital of Punjab State, in Pakistan and a decision was taken to create an entirely new city for its replacement rather than upgrade an existing one. In the spring of 1948, Chandigarh, a site at the foot of the Himalayas, was chosen. Initially the American architect Albert Mayer and his associate Matthew Nowicki were commissioned to plan the new capital but following Nowicki's sudden death in 1951, Le Corbusier was appointed as Architectural Advisor.

His Master Plan for the city laid out a vast grid of roads intersecting at right angles to form a series of substantially self-contained Sectors. Le Corbusier designed three Government buildings and the Open Hand sculpture, the symbol of the city, but the bulk of the buildings during the initial period, 1951-65, was the work of Corbusier's cousin, Pierre Jeanneret, and two British architects, Edwin Maxwell Fry and his wife, Jane Beverley Drew.

Planned for a population of some 150,000 rising to 500,000, this has risen to around 900,000 with another 350,000 in the satellite towns of S. A. S. Nagar in Punjab State and Panchkula in Haryana State. The City of Chandigarh is now an autonomous Union Territory, the capital of both the State of Punjab and of Haryana.

In common with all comparable developments in the city, when a new cinema is planned architects employed by the Municipal or State Authorities first produce a detailed control design to ensure that the building conforms with the precepts of the Architectural Master Plan. The site owner is obliged to complete the development adhering strictly to the approved scheme. Surprisingly, this system of regulation has not produced conformity; rather a succession of architects has found original expression working within the architectural controls, inspired, no doubt, by the built heritage around them.

Official intervention, however, does not stop there; all cinemas in the city must charge the same range of seat prices irrespective of how well or poorly appointed and how popular or otherwise the venue. With no allowance for inflation, very low ticket prices fixed many years ago by the Municipal Government have not been increased. Consequently, owners have had little incentive to undertake other than essential repairs and in recent years, despite a greatly increased population, no new cinemas have opened.

Kiran

Sector 22

Of the three principal architects working with Le Corbusier at Chandigarh, only Edwin Maxwell Fry designed a cinema for the new city. Fry (1899-1987) was born in Wallasey in Cheshire and studied under Professor Charles Reilly at Liverpool University. Initially favouring Neo-Georgian, he abandoned this style after embracing European Modernism in the early 1930s. One of the British pioneers of the International Style and a founder member of the MARS group, between 1934 and 1938 he was responsible for a number of important projects including private houses and blocks of flats in and around London. Later, in joint practice with his wife Jane Drew, Fry accepted commissions in several of the newly-emerging Commonwealth countries, where, as at Chandigarh, projects mostly involved housing, schools and colleges. Fry published *Fine Building* (1944), *Art in the Machine Age* (1969), and technical works on building in tropical climates. Two years after he retired in 1973, his memoirs, *Autobiographical Sketches*, appeared.

The Kiran was planned and built in 1954-56 during Chandigarh's initial phase of development as the centrepiece of one of the earliest local, or Sector-level, shopping areas. It presents a high curving roofline in dramatic contrast with the neighbouring low-rise terraces. A projecting hood-like canopy frames the façade of blue tiles surrounding a central block displaying an attraction poster. A thin asymmetrical canopy connects the cinema entrance to the roofline of the single-storey restaurant built along one side.

Inside, the doors, dados and pilasters are teak, most other surfaces plaster. The short but wide foyer is slightly curved and leads into the 552-seat auditorium comprising stalls and a small balcony. Indirectly illuminated, fibrous plaster plates on the ceiling curve down to join the large angled and overlapping boards along both side walls. Although decorative, this design has a functional purpose; it is part of the scheme of acoustic enhancement. The simple proscenium and bow-fronted stage have been retained, however, when the technical equipment was upgraded to 70mm Photophones with a DTS digital sound system, a new floating screen was installed without either masking or curtains. The restaurant, currently used as a storeroom, has all its original features: recessed ceiling lighting, wall mirrors and built-in tables and seats. Plans are in hand to re-open it after refurbishment.

↑ *The auditorium.*

→ *The exterior of the Kiran – the restaurant block is on the right.*

Jagat
Sector 17

After studying in Delhi and London, Aditya Prakash (b.1921) joined the team of architects working at Chandigarh, where he designed many projects in the new city including the Tagore Theatre (1961), which is generally recognised as his masterpiece. He was also responsible for the control design of three cinemas, the Jagat, the Neelam *(illustrated on page 41)* and the K.C. Being conversant with such technicalities as seating rakes, projection throws and acoustic requirements, Prakash was able to undertake these projects without recourse to specialist consultants.

Later, a Principal of the Chandigath College of Architecture (1967-82), Prakash has written three books about the city including the text of *Chandigarh: the City Beautiful* (1999). He continues to live in the city he helped to create.

At the Jagat, above a thin concrete canopy which extends the full width of the building, the façade is entirely filled with recessed glazing surmounted by a massive convex lintel and enclosed by a box-like, concrete frame.

Once inside, the style changes abruptly. The interior displays the characteristically lavish decoration of its designer, W. M. Namjoshi: walls and ceilings of swirling moulded plasterwork mostly painted pink, reeded wood panelling and modernist cylindrical chandeliers. The main foyer is a double-height space from where stairs with illuminated glass banisters rise to the balcony foyer; this serpentine-shaped gallery over the lower area is similarly enclosed. In the auditorium, which seats 952 on two levels, the walls are decorated with moulded relief blocks, some backlit, and the ceiling is a series of

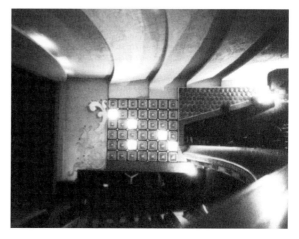

overlapping curved plates with recessed lighting. These finish as a proscenium around the Cinemascope screen. A drop curtain is present.

The cinema opened in 1958 with two Hi-Central Cinephonic/Simplex projectors, which are still in use after over forty years. Two Photophone 35s from Japan were added in c.1964 and in the 1990s, Dolby Sound. It programmes only Hindi films or dubbed versions of English-language pictures.

↑ *Part of the auditorium showing Namjoshi's scheme of illuminated panels and recessed ceiling lighting.*

→ *The façade of the Jagat. At the rear, the exterior has a similar canopy and area of glazing but no convex lintel.*

K. C.
Sector 17

Whilst remaining within the guidelines set out in Le Corbusier's Master Plan, Aditya Prakash was here allowed a freer hand than previously. The dramatic sculptural exterior consists of two massive, intersecting parabolic roofs rising from ground level; the result, the architect explained, of the building being designed from the inside out:

> ..... while working out the sight lines, acoustical forms and cinematographic projection for this design, I came to the following conclusions. There is no big requirement for a stage – just a screen; it is much better if projection of the film is as horizontal as possible and the form of the ceiling from the acoustical point of view leads to a curved shape.... I found a parabolic form of the roof will meet all requirements (and) at the same time the roof could be designed as a shell. The whole idea was for the roof form to float over the body of the cinema theatre.[38]

When building work started, Prakash was away from Chandigarh working on other projects and the plans were taken over by another architect appointed by the cinema's owner. Much to Prakash's regret, his "revolutionary scheme" for a 'floating' roof structure, that had been worked out with the engineer Dr Carbone, was abandoned; instead, an arrangement using reinforced concrete trusses was adopted to support a superimposed roof form.

The auditorium fills most of the main paraboloid, the 1,102 seats in a stepped layout on two floors. The projection box, with near-zero degree throw, has two Photophone 70/Superarc 35s and a stereo sound system.

Front of house facilities occupy the remainder of the main structure and the two transepts. A huge spiral ramp connects the open plan lobby and stalls foyer to the balcony level. Except for a restaurant added in 1997, the interior is unaltered

The unusual name of the cinema is derived from the initials of the owner, Kishan Chand. It opened on 3rd July 1971.

↑ Railings segregate male and female patrons at the ticket office windows – these echo the shape of the cinema exterior.

← The two intersecting parabolic roofs of the K.C.. The main entrance to the cinema is on the left; the steps on the right are additional access to the upper level foyer.

Batra
Sector 37

During the initial development stage of the new city, Harbinger Singh Chopra (1927-94) worked in the offices of both Le Corbusier and Pierre Jeanneret and later played a significant role in the architectural history of Chandigarth and more generally in the State of Punjab, including appointments as Principal of the Chandigarh College of Architecture and Senior Architect to the Punjab Agriculture University at Ludhiana. One of his major buildings is the Anglo-Sikh War Memorial at Ferozepur (1975). Strongly influenced by both European Masters, Chopra produced the control design for three cinemas in Chandigarh: the Batra and Nirman in the city and the Dhillon at the satellite development of Panchkula.

The Batra opened on 11 June 1980. Designed for the island site as a monumental statement employing both exposed *in-situ* and clad concrete surfaces, a wide slab parapet defines the footprint of the building above walls that are either deeply recessed or set at angles to the four outer faces of the structure. External ramps along one side of the building provide access to the balcony foyer.

Deeply recessed within the front façade, heavy hinged and sliding metal doors somewhat reminiscent of an American penitentiary allow access to a large, virtually unfurnished foyer. The walls and floors are of bare, unadorned concrete and except for small panels of brightly coloured ceramic tiles added later, there is no decoration. A row of glazed, parabola-shaped double doors along one side provides additional egress.

The comparable treatment of the balcony foyer has been compromised by the installation of strange, tree-like sculptures by Mohal Zulticar, presumably intended as homage to the work of Nek Chand at the famous Chandigarh Rock Garden. More examples of Zulticar's work are on display in the parking areas around the cinema.

With its 1,443-seats arranged in stalls and a balcony, the Batra is the largest cinema in the city. The auditorium is an elegant but purely functional space, decorated only by fretted and patterned acoustic panels carried right up to the edge of the screen. Projection equipment comprises two 70mm Westrex Hi-Lite projectors with a Dolby sound system.

→ *A side view of the Batra – a section of the external ramps is visible above and to the left of the three doors. The main entrance façade around the right hand corner presents a massive frame enclosing projecting and recessed blocks of doors and windows.*

↓ *The forbidding design of the metal doors and windows.*

Bassi

Sector 53
Sahibzada Ajit Singh Nagar

The Bassi Cinema Complex is the first twin-screen venue in the Chandigarh region. Within the one building, two parallel auditoria are designed with reverse orientation - in other words, siting the screens at opposite ends of the building. Unlike the usual multiscreen arrangement of common front of house areas and a shared projection cabin, this solution requires doubled facilities and additional staff. Notwithstanding the inevitable increased overheads, the scheme was selected as it would facilitate easy ingress and egress of large audience numbers from the two halls through two completely separate foyer areas.

Each auditorium contains 1,000 seats in stalls and a small balcony. To isolate the cinemas acoustically, a gap was left between the two, which is utilised for stairs and ramps connecting the two separate foyer areas at either end of the building. Double height passages along both exterior side walls further insulate the auditoria from external noise and provide pleasant areas for audience perambulation.

← The long façade of the Bassi. The entrance to one of the cinemas is under the arcade created by the overhang of the upper storeys.

Currently, both cinemas are equipped with 70mm Westrex projectors from America and Ultra stereo sound; the latter will be soon be upgraded to a Dolby system.

Of reinforced concrete with exposed shuttering marks, the massive rectangular structure is raised above ground level on cylindrical piloti. Around the perimeter, these are extended upwards as columns in front of large, deeply recessed areas of undulatory glazing and panels for attraction posters.

Although the population of S. A. S. Nagar is c.150,000, the Bassi Complex is the first cinema to be built in the satellite town. It opened on 15th January 1986. Located on an island site in a neighbourhood shopping centre, access to the two cinemas is through different entrances at either end of the building. Car parking space is provided in the open sub-basement.

Named after its owner, the Bassi was designed by the Chandigarh architect Sarbit Singh Bahga (b.1957) with interior design by the local firm of Gurmel Singh & Co.

274   Chandigarh

Suraj
Panchkula
Haryana State

Across the State border, a few kilometres outside Chandigarh beside the main highway to the North, is the Suraj, an out-of-town development surrounded by vast areas set aside for car parking. It was designed by the Chandigarh architect Vijay Malik of the Planners Group. This firm was responsible for the entire project, including all interior and technical specifications and has previously designed several other cinemas in the region. The Suraj opened in 1988.

Below a monumental parapet, the composition incorporates features found in earlier Chandigarh cinemas such as the massive coping, angled exterior walls and the extensive use of exposed concrete. Inside, the concrete, juxtaposed with areas of tiling and colour-washed plaster, is illuminated by subdued recessed lighting to create a series of interconnected, sculptural masses and voids. The foyer is a triple-height space into which the mezzanine and balcony foyers project. The cabin is placed one floor above. A row of thin cylindrical columns across the centre of the foyer rises the full three storeys passing through the foyer structures overhead. On the mezzanine level, a restaurant extends on to an open-air terrace situated behind one of the enormous circular windows in the outer walls of the building. Cylindrical towers at one side contain a spiral staircase and conveniences. The auditorium itself is virtually a building within a building and the spaces between its outer walls and the exterior walls of the structure are used as waiting areas or for offices. Inside the auditorium, which narrows sharply towards the screen, are 1,200 luxurious seats in stalls and a cantilevered balcony. Decoration is minimal; the floating screen almost fills one wall and has no decorative surround.

← *The Suraj - behind the large circular window is a terrace open to the sky.*

Glossary

Ajanta, caves of   see Ellora.

Atrium   Originally an inner court open to the sky, nowadays often with a glazed roof.

Bahadur   Literally brave: used as a title for those of high rank regardless of merit.

Auditorium   The area occupied by a seated audience during a performance at a theatre or cinema.

Bargeboard   Projecting board, often decorated or carved, on the edge of a gable.

Batter   Sloping wall face.

Brahmanism   Ancient Indian religion, a precursor of Hinduism.

Bhavan, Bhawan   A building or house.

Cantonment   A military camp or planned estate (esp. of the British period) situated on the periphery of a city. Effectively a suburb for the military and their families.

Chajja, Chhajja   A dripstone; a thin sloping projection of stone resembling a cornice.

Chhatri, Chattri   Literally an umbrella. A small pavilion or kiosk with open sides under a dome standing on piers. Often as a turret on a roof.

Chowk   Courtyard or square.

Coffering   Decoration on a ceiling, vault or arch soffit of sunken square or rectangular panels.

Crocket   A decorative feature of Gothic architecture comprising small projections from the angle of a spire.

Cupola   A small dome.

Durbar, Darbar   The court of a Princely State; a public audience given by a Ruler or Governor, in the British period by the Viceroy.

Ellora, caves of   Situated near Aurangabad, Madhya Pradesh. Decorated Hindu, Jain and Buddhist caves carved in volcanic rocks dating between 600 and 1100 A.D. Comparable but older caves are found at Ajanta, some 100 km North West.

Embrasure   An opening in a wall or recess for a door or window, usually angled.

Entablature   The upper part of a classical order incorporating architrave, frieze and cornice.

Haveli   A courtyard house.

Hood mould   A projecting stone over an arch of a window door, or opening.

Hindi   The principal Sanskrit-based language of India.

Howdah   A chair or framed seat on an elephant, may be elaborately decorated and canopied.

Independence (of India)   India became independent of British rule on 15th August 1947, when the country was partitioned into two self-governing Dominions – India and Pakistan. India became a Republic on 26th January 1950 remaining within the British Commonwealth.

Indo-Saracenic   A revivalist style of the late 19th and early 20th centuries employed by some British architects – a synthesis of Indian, principally Mughal, decorative details frequently employing traditional craft techniques and European building design.

Jali, Jaali   A pierced wooden or stone screen or lattice.

Jainism   Originally a reform movement of Brahmanism (q.v.), but exclusive to India. Jains revere all life and practise strict vegetarianism.

Khan   Honorific Muslim name or title.

Krishna   A popular incarnation of Vishnu – a God of Love, one of whose favourites is the milkmaid Radha (q.v.)

Lakshmi   The Goddess of Wealth, of Good Fortune - consort of Vishnu.

Languages (of India)   The Constitution of India recognises fifteen official languages. Hindi is predominant among the Hindu majority, Urdu among Muslims. Gujarat and Marathi are spoken in West India, Bengali in East India, Tamil and Tegulu in the South. The use of English is widespread amongst the educated classes throughout India.

Lines   A reference to the layout of an official or military colony under the British Raj, where each service was given its own area or roads, hence, Civil Lines, Military Lines etc.

Mahal   A mansion or palace.

Maharajah   A major Hindu Prince.

Maharani   The wife of a Maharajah.

Maidan   A large open, probably grassed space in a city or Town; a civic park.

Mandir   Originally a room, later a house or palace, latterly a temple.

Mandala   A geometric diagram symbolising the structure of the universe.

Mughal, Moghul   Applied to the architectural style developed in the 16th and 17th centuries during the reigns of Akbar and Shah Jehan and characterized by the integration of the Moorish arch with that of traditional Indian post and lintel construction.

Nautch   A dance performance.

Nawab   A Muslim aristocrat, nobleman, governor or ruler.

Nizam   The title of the hereditary Muslim rulers of the Princely State of Hyderabad.

Parsee, Parsi   Zoroastrian sect in Western India (esp. Mumbai) which escaped from persecution in Persia in the 9th century.

Partition   See Independence.

Piloti   Pillars or stilts used to raise a building to first-floor level, thereby leaving the ground-floor open.

Pilaster   A shallow column or pier attached to a wall.

Polychromy   The use of contrasting colours in a building.

Porte-cochère   A porch which permits vehicles to pass through.

Pradesh   A province.

Prakash   Light

Proscenium   In a theatre or cinema, the frame enclosing the stage or screen and separating it from the audience.

Punkah   A large fabric fan suspended from the ceiling operated by ropes.

Purdah   Literally a curtain – the system of seclusion of women from public view.

Pylon   Originally tower-like structures flanking the gateway of an ancient Egyptian temple; a narrow, vertical architectural feature.

Quatrefoil   Four leaf-shaped curves formed within a circle.

Radha   A milkmaid and favourite concubine of the God Krishna.

Raj   Rule, Government, Sovereignty; often applied to the period of British rule in India.

Rajah   A minor Hindu prince or nobleman.

Rajput   Literally Son of the Raja (King). Refers to the Kshatriyas or warrior caste of Hindus, mainly of Rajputana. (q.v.)

Rajputana   The Old name for Rajasthan, an area comprising twenty-two Princely States in North West India.

Rani   The wife of a rajah.

Quarry   Small panes of glass, usually quadrangular, originally used in Mediaeval lead glazing.

Sawai   Literally one and a quarter; a hereditary title of the Maharajah of Jaipur.

Shiva, Siva   In Hinduism, the three major aspects of the Supreme Being are descended in the 'Hindu Triad' consisting of Brahma the Creator, Vishnu the Preserver and Shiva the Destroyer and Reproducer.

Surya   The Sun, a male Diety. In Hindu art, the sun is usually represented as a dark red man riding in a chariot drawn by seven horses (the days of week). The charioteer is Aruna, literally the dawn.

Swastika, Satio, Sauvastika   An equilateral cross with arms bent at right angles; an ancient symbol of prosperity and good fortune which figures in many cultures long before its adoption by the National Socialist Party in Germany. In Hindu mythology, it is an auspicious sign representing night, magic, purity and the destructive Goddess Kali.

Tympanum   A recessed, ornamental panel between the lintel of a doorway and the arch above it.

Urdu   The principal language of Islamic Indians.

Verandah   A roofed porch or terrace along the side of a building.

Zenana   Secluded women's quarters. Rajput houses were divided into zenanas and mardanas (men's quarters).

References

1 Nair quoted in National Film Development Corporation 1998, p.2.

2 Alff, 1997, p.251.

3 Indian Cinematograph Committee, 1928.

4 Bhatt and Scriver, 1990, p.14.

5 Tillotson, 1989, p.131.

6 Dharap, 1977-78.

7 Harwood, 1999, p.2.

8 Armstead, 1987, p.192.

9 Chandavarkar quoted in Garga, 1996, p.51.

10 Indian Cinematograph Committee, 1928, quoted in Barnow and Krishnaswamy, 1980, p.46.; Landon, 1983, p.189.

11 Ray, quoted in Garga, 1996, p.30.

12 Sheppard, 1924, pp.110-122.

13 Regal Theatre, Bombay, Golden Jubilee Brochure, 1983.

14 Regal Theatre, Bombay, Inaugural Brochure, 1933.

15 Maneck Sidhwa quoted in Srirekha, 1990.

16 Dwivedi and Mehrotra, 2001, p.252.

17 Merchant quoted in Apsara Cinema Brochure, 1965.

18 Lewis, 1994, p.74.

19 Deming in *American Cinematographer*, June 1932, quoted in Garga, 1996, p.84.

20 Irving, 1981, p.129.

21 Dayal, 1988.

22 Serenyi, 1985, p.56.

23 Odeon, 1963, pp.15-17.

24 Schlanger quoted in Yeomans, 1967, p.172.

25 Theatre Catalog, 1953-54, pp. ix-xxxii.

26 Doshi quoted in White, 1993, p.118.

27 Correa, 1973, p.91.

28 British Council, 1992.

29 Davies, 1985, p.159.

30 Barr and Desmond, 1982, p.34.

31 Aryan Cinema . Video of Interview with son of Founder, c.1983. (Copy held at National Film Archive of India).

32 P. K. Nair, interviewed by authors in Pune, 2001.

33 Chaphalkar, 2000.

34 Armstead, 1987, p.90.

35 Prashant, 2001.

36 Holmes, 1995.

37 Ganga Theatre, 1932-44

38 Aditya Prakash, correspondence with the authors, 2000-01.

Bibliography

The principal books, journals and newspapers consulted:

Architectural Review (London).
Architecture & Design (New Delhi).
L'Architecture d'Aujourd'hui (Paris).
Asian Film Directory and Who's Who (Bombay).
Billboard (New York).
Bombay Builder (Bombay).
Bombay Gazette (Bombay).
Building News (London).
Cinema in India (Bombay).
Cinema Vision India (Bombay).
Design (New Delhi).
Film Comment (New York).
Film India (Bombay).
Film Monthly (Bombay).
Film World (Bombay).
Films and Filming (London).
India. A Reference Annual (New Delhi).
Indian Architect (Bombay).
Indian Builder (Bombay).
Indian Cinematograph Yearbook (Bombay).
The Indian Engineer (Calcutta).
Inside-Outside (Bombay).
Journal of the Royal Institute of British Architects (London).
Journal of the Indian Institute of Architects (Bombay).
Journal of the S.M.P.T.E. (Society of Motion Picture and Television Engineers) (White Plains, New York)
Kinematograph Weekly (London).
Kinematograph Yearbook (London).
Sight and Sound (London).
Theatre Catalog (Philadelphia).
Theatre World (Bangalore).
The Times of India (New Delhi).
Trade Guide (Bombay).
Variety (Hollywood).

Alff, Jon. *Art Deco. Gateway to Indian Modernism. Architecture-Design*, Nov-Dec 1991, pp 57-63.
Idem. *Temples of Light. Bombay's Art Deco Modern Myth. in* Rohatgi, P., Godrej, A., and Mehrotra, R. *Bombay to Mumbai Changing Perspectives*. 1st ed 1997. (Bombay: Marg).
Allen, Charles, and Dwidedi, Sharada. *Lives of the Indian Princes*. 1st ed 1984. (London: Century).
Apsara Cinema. Bombay's Latest Venue. Inaugural Souvenir Brochure 1965. Privately published.
Armstead, C. *Princely Pageant*. 1st ed 1987. (London: Thomas Harmsworth).
Atwell, David. Cathedals of the Movies. *A History of British Cinemas and Their Audiences*. 1st ed 1981. (London: Architectural Press).

Baghdadi, Rafique. *Bombay Theatres*. (undated MSS).
Bahga, Sarbit, Surinder and Yashinder. *Modern Architecture in India. Post-Independence Perspective*. 1st ed 1993. (New Delhi: Galgotia Publishing Co.)
Bahga, Sarbit and Surinder. *Le Corbusier and Pierre Jeanneret. Footprints in the Sands of Indian Architecture*. 1st ed 2000. (New Delhi: Galgotia Publishing Co.).
Barnouw, Erik, and Krishnaswamy, S. *Indian Film*. 2nd ed 1980. (New York: Oxford University Press).
Barr, P., and Desmond, R. Simla. *A Hill Station in British India*. Paperback edition 1982. (London: Scolar Press).
Bawden, Liz-Anne. *The Oxford Companion to Film*. 1st ed 1976. (London: OUP)
Bence-Jones, Mark. *Palaces of the Raj. Magnificence and Misery of the Lord Sahibs*. 1st ed 1973. (London: Allen and Unwin).
Idem. *The Viceroys of India*. 1st ed 1982. (London: Constable).
Beotra, B.R. *Law of the Cinematograph (Central States)*. 1st ed 1965. (New Delhi: Law Book Co.)
Bergeijk, H. van. *Willem Marinus Dudok. Architect-Stede-Bouwkundige* 1884-1874. 1st ed 1995. (Naarden: V and K Publishers).
Bhatt, Vikram, and Scriver, Peter. *After the Masters. Contemporary Indian Architecture*. 1st ed 1990. (Ahmedabad: Mapin).
Bluem, A. William, and Squire, Jason E. (Editors). *The Movie Business. American Film Industry Practice*. 1976. (New York: Hastings House).
British Council Building, New Delhi. Architectural Notes.1992. (New Delhi: British Council).
Burke, S. M., and Quraishi, Salim Al-Din. *The British Raj in India. An Historical Review*. 3rd imp 1997. (Karachi: OUP).
Burris-Meyer, Harold, and Cole, Edward C., *Theatres and Auditoriums. Progressive Architecture Library* 1st Ed 1949 (New York: Reinhold).

Ceram, C. W. *Archaeology of the Cinema*. 1st ed 1965. (London: Thames and Hudson).

Chabria, Suresh. *Light of India. Indian Silent Cinema 1912-1934.* 1ˢᵗ ed 1994. (New Delhi: Wiley Eastern).

Chaphalkar, Prakash. *How to Build a Multiscreen.* Theatre World (Asia). Jan-Mar 2000.

Idem. *The Multiplex Revolution. Cinema India Showspecial.* 2001 (Mumbai).

Chaudhuri, Sukanta. (Editor). *Calcutta: The Living City. Volume II: The Present and Future.* 1ˢᵗ paperback ed 1995. (Calcutta: Oxford University Press).

Cinema House, New Delhi: Master, Sathe and Kothari. Jnl Indian Inst Arch, May 1961. (re: Shiela, New Delhi).

Corea, Charles. *Bombay, India.* Architecture Plus, March 1973.

Crewe, Quentin. *The Last Maharaja. A Biography of Sawai Man Singh II.* 1ˢᵗ ed 1985. (London: Michael Joseph).

Cromie, Robert, et al. *Modern Cinemas.* 1st ed 1936. (London: Architectural Press).

Cunha, Uma da (Editor). *Indian Cinema '78/'79.* 1ˢᵗ ed 1979 (New Delhi: Rampal/Directorate of Film Festivals, Ministry of Information and Broadcasting).

Davies, Philip. *Splendours of the Raj. British Architecture in India 1660-1947.* 1ˢᵗ ed 1985. (London: John Murray).

Idem. *The Penguin Guide to the Monuments of India.* Volume II: *Islamic, Rajput, European.* 1ˢᵗ ed 1989. (Penguin Books).

Dayal, R. *My Reminiscences of Fifty Years.* in *Regal. New Delhi's Premier Theatre. Celebrating Golden Jubilee 1938-1988.* Supplement to Screen, 29th April 1988. (New Delhi).

Dharap, B. V. *Indian Films* 1972, yearly to 1979. (Bombay: Dharap Motion Picture Enterprises) 1983 yearly to 1985 (Pune: National Film Archive of India).

Dwivedi, Sharada, and Mehrotra, Rahul. *Fort Walks. Around Bombay's Fort Area.* 1ˢᵗ ed 1999. (Mumbai: Eminence Designs Pvt Ltd).

Idem. *Bombay. The Cities Within.* New ed 2001. (Mumbai: Eminence Designs Pvt Ltd).

The Elite Cinema, Calcutta. Jnl Indian Inst Arch, Jan-Mar 1951.

Evenson, Norma. *Chandigarh* (1966: Los Angeles: University of California Press).

Idem. *The Indian Metropolis.* 1ˢᵗ ed 1989. (New Haven and London: Yale University Press).

Fielding, Raymond. *A Technological History of Motion Pictures and Television.* 1ˢᵗ ed 1967. (Berkeley: University of California Press).

Filmistan Cinema, New Delhi: Master, Sathe and Kothari. Indian Builder, August 1957.

Frampton, Kenneth. *Charles Correa.* 1ˢᵗ ed 1996. (London: Thames and Hudson).

Fry, E. Maxwell. *Autobiographical Sketches.* 1ˢᵗ ed 1975. (London: Elek).

Ganga Theatre, Bikaner. The Office of Private Secretary of the Maharajah of Bikaner. Files 4450-4, 1932-44, documents in the Royal Archive.

Gangopadhyay, Promad. *The Unknown Calcutta: Grand Opera House.* Calcutta Skyline, Sept 1989.

Garga, B. D. *So Many Cinemas. The Motion Picture in India.* 1ˢᵗ ed 1996. (Bombay: Eminence Designs Ltd).

Globe, 1966. *Celebrating a Double Event. Gala Re-opening of the Globe, Calcutta and the Golden Jubilee of Globe Theatres (Pvt) Ltd, 1966.* (Privately published).

Gomery, D. *The Hollywood Studio System.* 1ˢᵗ ed 1986. (London: British Film Insitute/Macmillan).

Gradidge, Roderick. *In the Footsteps of Lutyens and Baker in India.* 1998 Tour Notes. (London: The Lutyens Trust).

Gray, Richard. *Cinemas in Britain. One Hundred Years of Cinema Architecture.* 1ˢᵗ ed 1996. (London: Lund Humphries).

Grover, Satish. *Building Beyond Borders. The Story of Contemporary Indian Architecture.* 1ˢᵗ ed 1995. (New Delhi: National Book Trust of India).

Gujral, Satish. *The World of Satish Gujral in his Own Words.* 1ˢᵗ ed 1993. (New Delhi: UBS Publishers).

Hall, Ben M. *The Best Remaining Seats. The Story of the Golden Age of the Movie Palace.* 1961 ed (New York: Bramhall).

Harding, C., and Popple, S. *A Companion to Early Cinema.* 1ˢᵗ ed 1996. (London: Cygnus Press).

Harwood, Elaine. *Picture Palaces. New Life for Old Cinemas.* 1ˢᵗ ed 1999. (London: English Heritage).

Holloway, David. *Playing the Empire. The Acts of the Holloway Touring Company.* 1ˢᵗ ed 1997. (London: Harrap).

Holmes, Fred, and Ann Newton. *Bridging Traditions. The Making of the Umaid Bhawan Palace.* 1ˢᵗ ed 1995. (New Delhi: Banyan Books).

Hulfish, David S. *Motion Picture Work. A General Treatise on Picture Taking, Picture Making, Photo-Plays, and Theater Management and Operation.* 1ˢᵗ ed 1913. (Chicago: American Technical Society).

Imperial Films 1926-1951. Silver Jubilee brochure. 1951 (Privately published).

Indian Cinematograph Committee. Report of Evidence 1928. (New Delhi: Government of India).

Indian Talkie 1931-1956. Silver Jubilee Souvenir. 1956. (New Delhi: Film Federation of India).

Irving, Robert Grant. *Indian Summer: Lutyens, Baker and Imperial Delhi.* 3ʳᵈ imp 1981. (New Haven and London: Yale University Press).

Iyer, Kamu. (Editor). *Buildings that Shaped Bombay. Works of G.B. Mhatre FRIBA.* 1ˢᵗ ed 2000. (Mumbai: Kamla Raheja Vidyanidhi Institute of Architecture).

Jaipur, Gayatri Devi, Maharani of. *A Princess Remembers.* Reprint 2000. (New Delhi: Rupa).

Jappelli, Paola, and Menna, Giovanni. *Willem Marinus Dudok Architetture & Citta 1884-1974.* 1st ed 1997. (Naples: Clean)

Jones, Bernard E. (Editor). *The Cinematograph Book. A Complete Practical Guide to the Taking and Projecting of Cinematograph Pictures.* Rev ed 1919. (London: Cassell).

Joshi, Kiran. *Documenting Chandigarh. The Indian Architecture of Pierre Jeanneret, Edwin Maxwell Fry and Jane Beverley Drew.* 1st ed 1999. (Ahmadabad: Mapin Publications).

Kabir, N. M. *Cinema in India: An Introductory Guide.* 1st ed 1991. (London: Museum of the Moving Image).

Kapur, Geeta. *Contemporary Indian Artists.* 1st ed 1979. (New Delhi: Bikas).

Katz, Ephraim. *The Film Encyclopedia.* 1st ed 1979. (New York: Putnam).

Kendal, Geoffrey. *The Shakespeare Wallah. The Autobiography.* 1st ed 1986. (London: Sidgwick and Jackson).

Landon, John W. *Behold the Mighty Wurlitzer. The History of the Theatre Pipe Organ.* 1st ed 1983. (Westport: Greenwood).

Lang, Jon, Desai, Madhavi, and Desai, Miki. *Architecture and Independence. The Search for Identity – India 1880-1980.* 1st ed 1997. (New Delhi: Oxford University Press).

Lent, John A. *The Asian Film Industry.* 1st ed 1990. (Austin: University of Texas Press).

Lewis, R. *The Life and Death of Peter Sellers.* 1st ed 1994. (London: Century).

Liberty Cinema, Bombay. *Gala Opening Souvenir Brochure,* 1950. (Privately published).

Lighthouse Cinema, Calcutta. Golden Jubilee Brochure, 1936-1956. (Privately published).

London, Christopher W. (Editor). *Architecture in Victorian and Edwardian India.* 1st ed 1994. (Mumbai: Marg Publications).

Maclean, J. M. *A Guide to Bombay 1875.* (Bombay Gazette).

Meloy, Arthur S., *Theatres and Motion Picture Houses. A Practical Treatise on the Proper Planning and Construction of Such Buildings and Containing Useful Suggestions, Rules and Data for the Benefit of Architects, Prospective Owners etc.* 1916. (New York: Architects Supply and Publishing).

McKeon, Elizabeth, and Everett, Linda. *Cinema Under the Stars. America's Love Affair with the Drive-In Movie Theater.* 1st ed 1998. (Nashville: Cumberland House).

Metcalf, Thomas R. *An Imperial Vision. Indian Architecture and Britain's Raj.* 1st ed 1989. (London: Faber).

Mishra, Ambarish. *Artistes Lament Opera House Closure.* Times of India, 3rd February 1991. (re: Royal Opera House, Mumbai).

Mittal. A. *Cinema Industry in India. Pricing and Taxation.* 1st ed 1995. (New Delhi: Industrial Publishing Co.).

Morris, Jan, and Winchester, Simon. *Stones of India. The Buildings of the Raj.* 1st ed 1983. (Oxford: OUP).

Muthiah, S. *Madras. The Gracious City.* 1st ed 1990. (Madras: Affiliated E-W Press).

National Film Development Corporation. *Indian Cinema: A Visual Voyage.* 1st ed 1998. (New Delhi: Ministry of Information and Broadcasting).

Naylor, David. *American Picture Palaces. The Architecture of Fantasy.* 1st Ed 1981. (New York. Van Nostrand and Reinhold).

Niggl, Reto. *Eckart Muthesius 1930. Der Palast des Maharadsches in Indore. The Maharajah's Palace in Indore. Architektur und Interieur. Architecture and Interior.* 1st ed 1996 (Stuttgart: Arnoldsche).

Odeon, 1963. *Additions and Alterations to Odeon Cinema, New Delhi.* Jnl Indian Inst Arch, Sept 1963.

Papadaki, Stamo. *Oscar Niemeyer.* 1st ed 1960. (New York: Braziller).

Patel, I. B. *Motion Picture Theatres in India.* Unpublished MSS in National Film Archive of India, Pune.

Patil, Vimla. *Bombay Mumbai.* Rev ed 2000. (Mumbai: Wilco).

Patnaik, Naveen. *A Desert Kingdom. The Rajputs of Bikaner.* 1st ed 1990. (London: Weidenfeld and Nicolson).

Pitt, Charles. *Opera in India.* in The New Grove Dictionary of *Opera.* 1st ed 1992. (London, Macmillan).

Idem. *Opera's Indian Spring - Parts I and II.* (London: Opera, July and August 2001).

Prakash, A., and V. *Chandigarh - The City Beautiful.* 1st ed 1999. (Chandigarh: Abhishek Publications).

Prasad, Shiv Nath. *I Think There Is A Story.* Exhibition catalogue note. (1967: University of Illinois).

Prashant, Sinha. *Cinema Halls Rush.* Times of India, 24th January 2001.

Pym, John. *The Wandering Company. Twenty-One Years of Merchant-Ivory Films.* 1st ed 1983. (London: British Film Institute/ New York: Museum of Modern Art).

Raheja, Dinesh, and Kothari, Jitendra. *The 100 Luminaries of Hindi Cinema.* 1st ed 1996. (Bombay: India Book House).

Rajadhyaksha, Ashish. *Indian Cinema: Origins to Independence.* in Nowell-Smith (Ed), *Oxford History of World Cinema.* 2nd ed 1996. (Oxford: Oxford University Press).

Rajadhyaksha, Ashish, and Willemen, Paul. *Encyclopaedia of Indian Cinema.* Rev ed 1999. (London: Fitzroy Dearborn).

Ramachandran, T. M. *Cinema India International.* (Bombay: 1985).

Rangoonwalla, Firoze. *A Pictorial History of Indian Cinema.* 1st ed 1979. (London: Hamlyn).

Rathbun, John B. *Motion Picture Making and Exhibiting. A Comprehensive Volume Treating the Principles of Motography: The Making of Motion Pictures: The Scenario: The Motion Picture Theater: The Projector: The Conduct of Film Exhibiting: Methods of Coloring Films: Taking Pictures, etc.* 1st Ed 1914. (New York: Thomson).

Raulet, Sylvie. *Maharaja's Palaces. European Style in Imperial India.* 1st ed 1997. (London: Philip Watson).

Regal Theatre, Bombay. The Theatre Magnificent. Inaugural Souvenir Brochure, 1933. (Privately published).

Regal Theatre, Bombay. Golden Jubilee Brochure 1983. (Privately published).

Reuben, Bunny. *Follywood Flashback. A Collection of Movie Memories.* 1st ed 1993. (New Delhi: Harper Collins India).

Richardson, F. H. *Motion Picture Handbook. A Guide for Managers and Operators of Motion Picture Theatres.* 3rd ed 1916 (New York: Moving Picture World).

Ricketson, Frank H. *The Management of Motion Picture Theatres.* 2nd Impr 1938. (New York: McGraw-Hill).

Robinson, Andrew. *Satyajit Ray. The Inner Eye.* 1st ed 1989. (London: Andre Deutsch).

Robinson, David. *World Cinema 1895-1980. A Short History.* 2nd rev ed 1981. (London: Eyre Methuen).

Rogers, Homi. *The Regal Sidhwas. Parsiana.* Vol 17, (1), 1994.

Royal Opera House, Bombay, Souvenir Book, see Sheppard, J. J. (1924).

Russell, H. *An Architect's Progress: Thomas White Lamb.* Marquee, Journal of the Theatre Historical Society of America. Volume 21, (1), (1989).

Sarkar, Shiladitya. *Halls Beware! Queue for Tickets is Getting Shorter.* The Times of India. 7th February 2000. Calcutta Supplement.

Schlanger, 1953-54. *The Accomplishments of Ben Schlanger, Architect; Ben Schlanger Theories and Practices.* Theatre Catalog 1953-54 Annual.

Ben Schlanger. Jnl SMPTE, Vol 79, 1970.

Ben Schlanger: Obituary Notice. Jnl SMPTE, Vol 80,1971.

Serenyi, Peter. *From Lutyens to Young Indian Architecture: 60 Years of Housing in New Delhi.* Techniques and Architecture, Aug-Sep 1985.

Sethi, Sunil. *Interieurs de l'Inde, Indian Interiors, Indien Interieurs.* c.1995. (Köln: Taschen)

Sexton, R. W., and Betts B. F. *American Theatres of Today, illustrated with Plans, Sections and Photographs of Exterior and Interior Details of Modern Motion Picture and Legitimate Theatres Throughout the United States Volume 1.* 1st ed 1927; *Volume 2.* 1st ed 1930. (New York: Architectural Book Publishers). (Volume 2 includes an article by Ben Schlanger on cinema design)

Shah, Panna. *The Indian Film.* 1st ed 1950. (Bombay: Motion Picture Society of India).

Shand, P. Morton. *The Architecture of Pleasure 1: Modern Theatres and Cinemas.* 1st ed 1930. (London: Batsford).

Sharp, Dennis. *The Picture Palace and Other Buildings for the Movies.* 1st ed 1969. (London: Evelyn).

Sheppard, J. J. (Editor). *Vivid Glimpses of India.* 1st ed 1924. (Bombay: J. F. Karaka, Royal Opera House).

Shiela Commemorative Booklet 1971. (Privately published).

Singh, Dhananajaya. *Marwar Jodhpur.* 1st ed 1996. (New Delhi: Banyan Books).

Srirekha, N.C. *Romance of the Regal.* Mid-Day, Bombay. 30th March 1990.

Sloane, T. O'Connor. *Motion Picture Projection.* 1st ed 1922. (New York: Falk).

Stamp, Gavin. *Indian Summer.* The Architectural Review, June 1976.

Steele, James. *The Complete Architecture of Balkrishna Doshi. Re-thinking Modernism for the Developing World.* 1st ed 1998. (London: Thames and Hudson).

Stein, Elliot. *Film India.* Film Comment, Jul-Aug 1981.

Stoddard, Richard. *Theatre and Cinema Architecture. A Guide to Information Sources.* 1st ed 1978. (Detroit: Gale Research).

Stones, Barbara. *America Goes to the Movies. 100 Years of Motion Picture Exhibition.* 1st ed 1993. (North Hollywood: National Association of Theatre Owners).

Sugich, Michael. *Palaces of India.* 1st ed 1992. (London: Pavilion).

Thomas, P. Epics, *Myths and Legends of India. A Comprehensive Survey of the Sacred Lore of the Hindus, Buddhists and Jains.* 13th ed 1973. (Bombay: Taraporevala).

Thoraval, Yves. *The Cinemas of India. 1896-2000.* 1st ed 2000. (New Delhi: Macmillan India Ltd).

Thorne, Ross. *Cinemas of Australia via USA.* 1st ed 1981. (Sydney: Architecture Dept, University of Sydney).

Tillotson, G. H. R. *The Tradition of Indian Architecture.* 1st ed 1989. (New Haven and London: Yale University Press).

Times of India. Flashback. Sesquicentennial 1840-1990. 1990 1st ed. (Bombay: Times of India).

Tindall, Gillian. *City of Gold. The Biography of Bombay.* 1st ed 1982. (London: Temple Smith).

Usai, Paolo Cherchi. *Burning Passions. An Introduction to the Study of Silent Cinema.* 2nd Impr. 1995. (London: British Film Institute).

Valicha, Kishore. *The Moving Image. A Study of Indian Cinema.* 1st ed 1988. (Bombay: Orient Longmans).

Vaughan, P. (Editor). *The Victoria Memorial Hall, Calcutta.* 1st ed 1977. (Calcutta: Marg Publications).

White, Stephen. *Building in the Garden. The Architecture of Joseph Allen Stein in India and California.* 1st ed 1993. (New Delhi: Oxford University Press).

Work in Progress: Cinema at Curzon Road, New Delhi. Jnl Indian Inst Arch, Oct-Dec 1964. (re: the unbuilt cinema designed by Prasad).

Yeomans, *John. The Other Taj Mahal. What Happened to the Sydney Opera House.* 1st ed 1967. (London: Nelson).

Index

The names of Indian cinemas are shown in capitals.